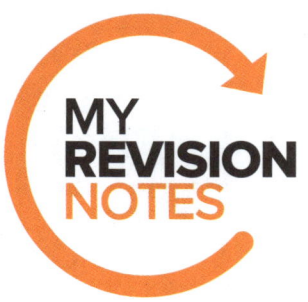

Cambridge National

Level 1/Level 2

SPORT STUDIES
SECOND EDITION

For the J829 specification

Symond Burrows
Sue Young

Picture credits

page 10 © l.glz.ttlphotos /Shutterstock.com; **page 17** © Microgen / stock.adobe.com; **page 18** © JackF / stock.adobe.com; **page 21** © Africa Studio / stock.adobe.com; **page 23** © Kaspars Grinvalds / stock.adobe.com; **page 26** © Esteban Martinena Guerrero / Alamy Stock Photo; **page 27** © nenetus / stock.adobe.com; **page 30** © Leonard Zhukovsky / 123 RF; **page 33** © Anthony Devlin / PA Images / Alamy Stock Photo; **page 40** © RedCap / Shutterstock.com; **page 43** © Zita Stankova / Shutterstock.com; **page 45** © Chris Jackson / Getty Images; **page 49** © Stu Forster / Getty Images; **page 59** © Marco Ciccolella; **page 67** © lev radin / Shutterstock.com

Every effort has been made to trace all copyright holders, but if any have been inadvertently overlooked, the Publishers will be pleased to make the necessary arrangements at the first opportunity.

Although every effort has been made to ensure that website addresses are correct at time of going to press, Hodder Education cannot be held responsible for the content of any website mentioned in this book. It is sometimes possible to find a relocated web page by typing in the address of the home page for a website in the URL window of your browser.

Hachette UK's policy is to use papers that are natural, renewable and recyclable products and made from wood grown in well-managed forests and other controlled sources. The logging and manufacturing processes are expected to conform to the environmental regulations of the country of origin.

Orders: please contact Hachette UK Distribution, Hely Hutchinson Centre, Milton Road, Didcot, Oxfordshire, OX11 7HH. Telephone: +44 (0)1235 827827. Email education@hachette.co.uk. Lines are open from 9 a.m. to 5 p.m., Monday to Friday. You can also order through our website: www.hoddereducation.co.uk

ISBN: 978 1 3983 5118 9

© Symond Burrows and Sue Young 2022

First published in 2020
This edition published in 2022 by
Hodder Education,
An Hachette UK Company
Carmelite House
50 Victoria Embankment
London EC4Y 0DZ

www.hoddereducation.co.uk

Impression number   10 9 8 7 6 5 4 3 2

Year   2025 2024

All rights reserved. Apart from any use permitted under UK copyright law, no part of this publication may be reproduced or transmitted in any form or by any means, electronic or mechanical, including photocopying and recording, or held within any information storage and retrieval system, without permission in writing from the publisher or under licence from the Copyright Licensing Agency Limited. Further details of such licences (for reprographic reproduction) may be obtained from the Copyright Licensing Agency Limited, www.cla.co.uk

Cover photo: © Petr Malyshev – stock.adobe.com

Typeset in India

Printed in Spain

A catalogue record for this title is available from the British Library.

Get the most from this book

This book will help you to revise for your Cambridge National in Sport Studies exam (Unit R184: Contemporary issues in sport). You can find out more about the exam on pages 7 and 8.

Everyone has to decide his or her own revision strategy, but it is essential to review your work, learn it and test your understanding. These Revision Notes will help you to do that in a planned way, topic by topic. Use this book as the cornerstone of your revision and don't hesitate to write in it: personalise your notes and check your progress by ticking off each section as you revise.

Tick to track your progress

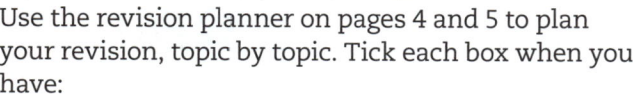

Use the revision planner on pages 4 and 5 to plan your revision, topic by topic. Tick each box when you have:
+ revised and understood a topic
+ tested yourself
+ practised exam questions.

You can also keep track of your revision by ticking off each topic heading in the book. You may find it helpful to add your own notes as you work through each topic.

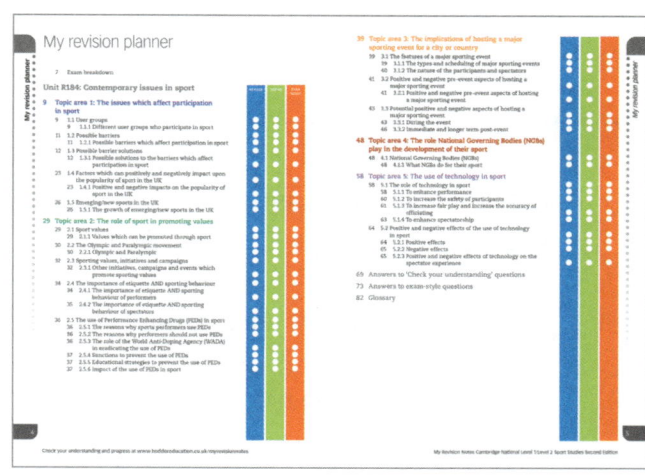

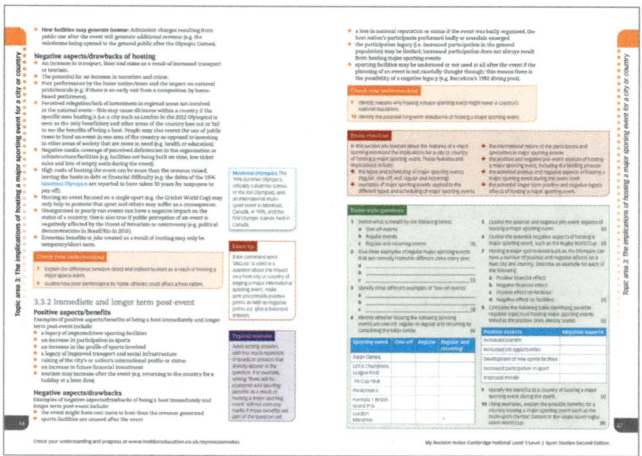

Features to help you succeed

Exam tips
Expert tips to help you polish your exam technique and maximise your chances in the exam.

Typical mistakes
Common mistakes made by other students and guidance on how to avoid them.

Check your understanding
Short questions to test your knowledge and understanding as you work through the course. Answers are given at the back of the book.

Now test yourself
Revision activities to guide your note-taking.

Definitions and key words
Clear, concise definitions of essential-to-know terms.

Exam-style questions
Practice exam questions. Use them to consolidate your revision and practise your exam skills. Answers are given at the back of the book.

My Revision Notes Cambridge National Level 1/Level 2 in Sport Studies Second Edition

My revision planner

7 Exam breakdown

Unit R184: Contemporary issues in sport

9 Topic area 1: The issues which affect participation in sport

- 9   1.1 User groups
  - 9   1.1.1 Different user groups who participate in sport
- 11   1.2 Possible barriers
  - 11   1.2.1 Possible barriers which affect participation in sport
- 12   1.3 Possible barrier solutions
  - 12   1.3.1 Possible solutions to the barriers which affect participation in sport
- 23   1.4 Factors which can positively and negatively impact upon the popularity of sport in the UK
  - 23   1.4.1 Positive and negative impacts on the popularity of sport in the UK
- 26   1.5 Emerging/new sports in the UK
  - 26   1.5.1 The growth of emerging/new sports in the UK

29 Topic area 2: The role of sport in promoting values

- 29   2.1 Sport values
  - 29   2.1.1 Values which can be promoted through sport
- 30   2.2 The Olympic and Paralympic movement
  - 30   2.2.1 Olympic and Paralympic
- 32   2.3 Sporting values, initiatives and campaigns
  - 32   2.3.1 Other initiatives, campaigns and events which promote sporting values
- 34   2.4 The importance of etiquette AND sporting behaviour
  - 34   2.4.1 The importance of etiquette AND sporting behaviour of performers
  - 35   2.4.2 The importance of etiquette AND sporting behaviour of spectators
- 36   2.5 The use of Performance Enhancing Drugs (PEDs) in sport
  - 36   2.5.1 The reasons why sports performers use PEDs
  - 36   2.5.2 The reasons why performers should not use PEDs
  - 36   2.5.3 The role of the World Anti-Doping Agency (WADA) in eradicating the use of PEDs
  - 37   2.5.4 Sanctions to prevent the use of PEDs
  - 37   2.5.5 Educational strategies to prevent the use of PEDs
  - 37   2.5.6 Impact of the use of PEDs on the sport

Check your understanding and progress at www.hoddereducation.co.uk/myrevisionnotes

39 Topic area 3: The implications of hosting a major sporting event for a city or country
    39 3.1 The features of a major sporting event
        39   3.1.1 The types and scheduling of major sporting events
        40   3.1.2 The nature of the participants and spectators
    41 3.2 Positive and negative pre-event aspects of hosting a major sporting event
        41   3.2.1 Positive and negative pre-event aspects of hosting a major sporting event
    43 3.3 Potential positive and negative aspects of hosting a major sporting event
        43   3.3.1 During the event
        46   3.3.2 Immediate and longer term post-event

48 Topic area 4: The role National Governing Bodies (NGBs) play in the development of their sport
    48 4.1 National Governing Bodies (NGBs)
        48   4.1.1 What NGBs do for their sport

58 Topic area 5: The use of technology in sport
    58 5.1 The role of technology in sport
        58   5.1.1 To enhance performance
        60   5.1.2 To increase the safety of participants
        61   5.1.3 To increase fair play and increase the accuracy of officiating
        63   5.1.4 To enhance spectatorship
    64 5.2 Positive and negative effects of the use of technology in sport
        64   5.2.1 Positive effects
        65   5.2.2 Negative effects
        65   5.2.3 Positive and negative effects of technology on the spectator experience

69 Answers to 'Check your understanding' questions

73 Answers to exam-style questions

82 Glossary

Countdown to my exam

6–8 weeks to go

- Start by looking at the specification – make sure you know exactly what material you need to revise and the style of the examination. Use the revision planner on pages 4 and 5 to familiarise yourself with the topics.
- Organise your notes, making sure you have covered everything on the specification. The revision planner will help you to group your notes into topics.
- Work out a realistic revision plan that will allow you time for relaxation. Set aside days and times for all the subjects that you need to study, and stick to your timetable.
- Set yourself sensible targets. Break your revision down into focused sessions of around 40 minutes, divided by breaks. These Revision Notes organise the basic facts into short, memorable sections to make revising easier.

REVISED

4–6 weeks to go

- Read through the relevant sections of this book and refer to the 'remember' tips, key terms, summaries and exam skills. Tick off the topics as you feel confident about them. Highlight those topics you find difficult and look at them again in detail.
- Test your understanding of each topic by working through the 'Now test yourself' questions in the book. Look up the answers at the back of the book.
- Make a note of any problem areas as you revise, and ask your teacher to go over these in class.
- Look at past papers. They are one of the best ways to revise and practise your exam skills. Write or prepare planned answers to the exam style questions provided in this book.
- Try using different revision methods as you work through the sections. For example, you can make notes using mind maps, spider diagrams or flash cards.
- Track your progress using the revision planner and give yourself a reward when you have achieved your target.

REVISED

One week to go

- Try to fit in at least one more timed practice of an entire past paper and seek feedback from your teacher, comparing your work closely with the mark scheme.
- Check the revision planner to make sure you haven't missed out any topics. Brush up on any areas of difficulty by talking them over with a friend or getting help from your teacher.
- Attend any revision classes put on by your teacher. Remember, your teacher is an expert at preparing people for examinations.

REVISED

The day before the examination

- Flick through these Revision Notes for useful reminders, for example the 'remember' tips, key terms, summaries and exam skills.
- Check the time and place of your examination.
- Make sure you have everything you need – extra pens and pencils, tissues, a watch, bottled water and sweets.
- Allow some time to relax and have an early night to ensure you are fresh and alert for the examination.

REVISED

My exams

Unit R184 paper

Date: ....

Time: ....

Location: ....

Check your understanding and progress at www.hoddereducation.co.uk/myrevisionnotes

Exam breakdown

About the exam

Unit R184 Contemporary issues in sport is the only exam-based unit on the OCR Level 1/Level 2 Cambridge National in Sport Studies and it counts for 40 per cent of your overall qualification weighting. It is important to understand the content to be covered, how the exam is structured and the different types of questions you are likely to face.

Unit R184 Contemporary issues in sport covers a range of topical and contemporary issues that broadly relate to five separate topic areas, all covered in this revision book:
1. Participation levels of different user groups and barriers/solutions to barriers which affect participation
2. Promotion of values and ethical behaviour through sport
3. The role of high-profile sporting events and the implications of hosting a major sports event for a city or country
4. The role of National Governing Bodies (NGBs) in the development of a sport
5. How technology is being used in sport (by performers, officials and fans).

The paper is 1 hour and 15 minutes long and is worth 70 marks. When looking at the exam board specification outlining these, it is important to be aware that the breadth and depth column identifies some topics as requiring 'knowledge only'.

Knowledge = the ability to **'identify'** or recognise something (e.g. from a diagram); it requires the ability to use 'direct recall' in order to answer a question (e.g. define a term). Two examples of knowledge requirements in the specification are:
+ know the user groups
+ know the Olympic Creed, Olympic symbol, and Olympic and Paralympic values.

All other topics will require both knowledge **and** understanding.

Understanding = the ability to **assess and evidence** the perceived meaning of something to illustrate your depth of understanding. It requires an ability to answer questions with words such as:
+ how
+ why
+ when
+ reasons for
+ benefits and drawbacks of
+ advantages and disadvantages of
+ purpose of
+ suitability of
+ recommendations for improvement include
+ pros and cons of
+ the appropriateness of something to.

Structure of the exam paper

The exam paper is divided into three sections:

Section A is worth 30 marks and contains **multiple-choice questions** and **short answer questions** with a focus on **Performance Objective (PO) 1 (recall knowledge and show understanding of sport studies concepts)**. Questions in this section may ask you to 'state' or 'identify' something (e.g. *State* one national sporting initiative; *Identify* a major sporting event).

Exam breakdown

Section B (worth 28 marks) and Section C (worth 12 marks) include short- and medium-answer questions which are focused more on P02 (application of knowledge and understanding of sport studies concepts), with some P01. These questions may ask you to provide practical examples to illustrate application of knowledge and understanding (e.g. Using practical examples, describe three different ways in which a sports performer can show sportsmanship; Using named sports as examples, outline two different examples of good spectator etiquette).

The final question, contained at the end of Section C of the exam paper, will be an 'extended response' P03 question (analysis and evaluation of knowledge, understanding and performance) (e.g. Discuss the reasons why countries may wish to bid for and host the football World Cup). This question needs to be answered in more depth and is assessed against a 'levels of response' mark scheme. To achieve the highest level your answer needs to be well-structured and you must use correct spelling, punctuation and grammar and specialist terminology where it is appropriate.

Command words used in Unit R184 Contemporary issues in sport exam questions:

- **Analyse** – Separate or break down information into parts and identify their characteristics or elements
- **Annotate** – Add information, for example, to a table, diagram or graph until it is final
- **Calculate** – Get a numerical answer showing how it has been worked out
- **Choose** (Which one of the following?) – Select an answer from options given
- **Circle** – Select an answer from the options given
- **Compare and contrast** – Give an account of the similarities and differences between two or more items or situations
- **Complete** – Add all the needed or appropriate parts; Add information, for example, to a table, diagram or graph until it is final
- **Describe** – Give an account including all the relevant characteristics, qualities or events; Give a detailed account of …
- ***Discuss** – Present, analyse and evaluate relevant points (for example, for/against an argument)
- **Draw** – Produce a picture or diagram
- **Evaluate** – Make a reasoned qualitative judgement considering different factors and using available knowledge/experience
- ***Explain** – Give reasons for and/or causes of; Use the words 'because' or 'therefore' in answers
- **Fill in** – Add all the needed or appropriate parts; Add information, for example, to a table, diagram or graph until it is final
- ***Identify** – Give an answer to answer the question set; Select an answer from options given; Recognise, name or provide factors or features
- **Justify** – Give good reasons for offering an opinion or reaching a conclusion
- **Label** – Add information, for example, to a table, diagram or graph until it is final; Add all the necessary or appropriate parts
- **Outline** – Give a short account, summary or description
- ***State** – Give factors or features; Give short, factual answers (often linked to a specific number in the question)
- ***Using practical examples** – Show your full understanding of points being made by using relevant practical/sporting examples linked to the requirements of the question set

* = commonly used command words in the Contemporary Issues exam paper you particularly need to be aware of and be able to respond correctly to

Topic area 1: The issues which affect participation in sport

1.1 User groups

REVISED

1.1.1 Different user groups who participate in sport

There are a range of different user groups who participate in sport. Some user groups face the possible barriers which affect their participation. There are a range of possible barrier solutions to help solve the relative lack of participation of each group when compared to other sections of society (e.g. women compared to men, and people with disabilities compared to non-disabled people).

Table 1.1 User groups who participate in sport

User group	Explanation
Gender	The state of identifying as either male or female (although this can be a sliding scale). Sometimes different genders have different needs, goals and requirements for sport which may or may not be met to enable participation to take place, or not as the case may be.
People from different ethnic groups	People of different ethnicities have different needs and requirements in order for their sporting needs to be met. Those who are not from the majority ethnic group in a country or those within a community that is of a different nationality, culture or religion from the main group in that area or country are particularly likely to participate in lower numbers than their societal counterparts.
Retired people/people over 60	People over the age of 60, many of whom do not/no longer work and are possibly in receipt of a work or state pension
Families with children	Parents or carers who look after children of various ages, some of whom may not be old enough to attend school
Carers	Adults or children caring for relatives, elderly parents or siblings
People with family commitments	Adults who are raising a family/children without a partner
Young children	From birth to the end of primary school (i.e. 0–11 years old)
Teenagers	Individuals of compulsory secondary school age (i.e. from 11 through to 16 years of age)
People with disabilities	Individuals with a range of different types of disability including those with a physical, sensory or mental condition that affects or limits their senses, movements or ability to do certain activities
Parents (singles or couples)	Single parents or couples with children as dependents
People who work	Individuals who are in employment
Unemployed/economically disadvantaged people	Individuals who do not have a paid job and/or have a low-income level

> **User groups** A number of people who are classed together with the same interests who use a product (e.g. a fitness class at a sports centre) and may face a variety of barriers to their participation in sports.
>
> **Participate/participation** Taking part.
>
> **Gender** A term used to describe the characteristics of men and women which are socially constructed.
>
> **Ethnic group** A social group that has a common national or cultural tradition.
>
> **Culture** The rules, customs and beliefs of a particular group or society.
>
> **Retired people** Individuals who have withdrawn from their active working life and are no longer employed in an occupation.
>
> **Economically disadvantaged** Someone who does not have enough income to meet basic needs and qualifies for state-organised benefits.

Figure 1.1 Young girl playing goalball, a sport where vision is not required to participate

Exam tip

Make sure you know and can list the twelve different user groups who participate in sport identified on the syllabus. To gain the most marks, you will need to apply your knowledge of these groups in a relevant way to any scenarios or examples that may be given in an exam question.

Now test yourself

TESTED

Draw a table or spider diagram to show the twelve different user groups referred to in the specification, with a brief explanation of who they are (1–6 at the top and 7–12 at the bottom if using a spider diagram). Memorise the user groups so that you can pick the most appropriate one from the list and apply it to a given scenario in an exam question.

Check your understanding

1 Who might child or adult carers be required to look after?
2 Identify three different types of disability which impact on participation in physical activity and sport.

Typical mistake

Many students mention irrelevant user groups in their answers to exam question scenarios, which means relatively easy marks are lost. In terms of people with disabilities, there is sometimes too narrow a focus on physical disabilities and wheelchair users. Instead try to show awareness of a range of disabilities in your answers.

1.2 Possible barriers

1.2.1 Possible barriers which affect participation in sport

It is important to appreciate that not everyone in society has an unlimited choice of when and where they might participate in physical activity and sport. A number of barriers to participation exist which negatively impact on user group participation, as explained in Table 1.2 below.

Table 1.2 Barriers to participation

Possible barrier affecting participation in sport	Explanation/example of this barrier and its negative impact on participation
Employment and unemployment	Being employed can be demanding in terms of long working hours, but not having a job might cause individuals to have low incomes, in addition to low levels of motivation to participate
Family commitments	Looking after children can be very demanding and expensive, which can leave little time or money for participating in sport.
Lack of disposable income	Taking part in sport often has costs attached to it which lots of user groups/people are unable to afford (e.g. equipment and membership costs)
Lack of transport	Not having a driving licence and/or vehicle access to enable people to travel to sporting locations sometimes hinders participation
Lack of positive sporting role models	People we admire and who inspire others to be like them are sometimes lacking for various user groups when it comes to sports participation
Lack of positive family role models or family support	Parental and sibling encouragement or inspiration to take part in sport may be lacking in various user groups
Lack of appropriate activity provision	Different user groups require activity sessions to be well thought through and planned well in advance to help ensure the sessions meet their varied needs and requirements
Lack of awareness of appropriate activity provision	Some people do not know their local area well or the activities or club provision available to them, which can have a negative impact on participation
The lack of equal coverage in media in terms of gender and ethnicity	Some user groups do not receive representative coverage in the media when it comes to sporting events. People may be put off by stereotypical images – portraying people of particular genders or ethnicities in a negative way – and some groups may see themselves less often in sports coverage/reporting or be affected by the gender/ethnicity imbalance in sport punditry.

Barriers to participation Things that stop or limit an individual from participating in or developing their skills in a physical activity or sport.

Disposable income The amount of money a person has left over to spend on non-essentials once all their financial commitments have been met (paying food bills, paying the mortgage, etc.).

Role model A person viewed by others as an example to be imitated.

Sport punditry The provision of expertise (i.e. advice/information) in sport.

1.3 Possible barrier solutions

1.3.1 Possible solutions to the barriers which affect participation in sport

There are a number of possible solutions to the nine barriers in Table 1.2. These are outlined in Table 1.3.

Table 1.3 Possible barrier solutions

Possible barrier affecting participation in sport	Possible solutions to this barrier
Employment and unemployment	Employed people may require provision of sessions at appropriate times to fit around their working commitments
	Unemployed people may require appropriate pricing (e.g. **concessions**, free or reduced-price equipment)
Family commitments	Provision of appropriate sessions at flexible times to suit people who are very busy
Lack of disposable income	Appropriate pricing for all user groups (e.g. concessions, **taster sessions** and free or reduced-price equipment)
Lack of transport	To improve access to sports facilities, increased and appropriate or adapted transport needs to be provided (e.g. taxis/minibuses with wheelchair access)
Lack of positive sporting role models	Promote participation by increasing exposure to positive and inspirational role models
Lack of positive family role models or family support	Educate parents and family members on the benefits of sport to help provide a mutually supportive environment in which physical activity is encouraged
Lack of appropriate activity provision	Carefully consider and plan sporting provision (e.g. appropriate programmes, sessions, appealing activities and times for different user groups)
	Provision of appropriate facilities and equipment such as ramps, hearing loops for deaf users or braille signage for partially sighted users
Lack of awareness of appropriate activity provision	Carefully consider the promotional strategies being used and ensure that a range of different ways to promote activities are used (e.g. via targeted promotion, use of role models, advertisements, and initiatives and incentives such as taster sessions)
The lack of equal coverage in the media in terms of gender and ethnicity	Use media coverage to challenge stereotypical images (e.g. of 'gender appropriate' activities via women's rugby, boxing, etc.); ensure a varied cross-section of gender and ethnic groups are employed as sports pundits

> **Check your understanding**
>
> 3 How could being unemployed act as a barrier to participation in sport?
> 4 Identify the barrier that links to the inability to access and/or drive a vehicle to enable participation to take place.
> 5 What are the possible solutions to a lack of disposable income as a barrier to participation?

Concessions Discounts off full-price admissions for selected groups (e.g. school students).

Taster sessions Sessions in which you work for free or at a reduced rate to introduce yourself to potential clients (e.g. a fitness class or first introduction to a sport).

Check your understanding and progress at www.hoddereducation.co.uk/myrevisionnotes

Barriers impacting user group participation and possible solutions

It is important to be able to apply your knowledge of barriers to participation and possible solutions directly to different user groups, as explained below.

Gender

Different genders may have different needs, goals and requirements for sport. Often, these needs are not met. For women in particular there are a range of potential barriers that can impact their ability to participate in sport. These are illustrated in Table 1.4 below, which also suggests various solutions to these barriers.

> **Stereotypes** Widely held but fixed and oversimplified images or ideas of a particular type of person or thing.

Table 1.4 Possible barriers to female sport participation with solutions

Barriers	Example/explanation of barriers	Possible solutions to these barriers
Employment demands	Working long hours can leave limited time and/or energy for sport	Provide activities at times to suit such women
Family commitments	Many women still assume the role of primary caregiver to their children, which can leave them with little time or money to participate in sport; alternatively, any time or money available may be devoted to allowing the children to participate in sport, leaving the women unable to participate themselves	Provide activities at appropriate times and lower prices for women with children; provide crèche facilities or activities that all the family can do together
Lack of disposable income	Many women earn lower levels of pay compared to their male counterparts and there are often longer working hours in many traditionally 'female' occupations (e.g. the health and care sector)	Ensure appropriate pricing (e.g. concessions for women)
Lack of positive sporting role models	Limited media coverage of women's sport due to assumptions about lower audience interest and continued traditional **stereotypes** of women's childcare role and/or domestic responsibilities	Increase media coverage of women's sport and use of promotional strategies/campaigns such as Sport England's 'This Girl Can' campaign, which shows ordinary women and girls participating in sport, enabling this target group to identify with role models who are 'just like them', promoting participation
Lack of appropriate activity provision (e.g. due to existing stereotypes)	Women may not always be able to access the sports/activities they wish to participate in (e.g. if the sports are assumed not to be 'female appropriate' activities, as in the case of boxing and weightlifting, which require aggression and power – traits which are often stereotypically associated with masculinity)	Ensure all activities are made accessible and available to women
Lack of awareness of appropriate activity provision	Local knowledge of what activities are available for them to join in with may be lacking	Use a range of promotional strategies to improve knowledge and awareness of activity provision for women (e.g. social media advertisements)
Lack of equal coverage in the media in terms of gender, as well as gender imbalance in sport punditry	There is still less media coverage of women's sport compared with men's which negatively impacts on possible opportunities for sponsorship and/or full-time sporting opportunities	Increase media coverage of women's sport and the use of female pundits on sports programmes (e.g. Claire Balding, Gabby Yorath and Alex Scott.)

People from different ethnic groups

People from minority ethnic groups often face a number of barriers to participation, meaning that they are less likely to be involved in sports or certain activities. These barriers are explored in Table 1.5.

Table 1.5 Possible barriers to sport participation for minority ethnic groups, with solutions

Barriers	Example/explanation of barriers	Possible solutions to these barriers
Family commitments/ religious restrictions	**Cultural norms** may mean traditional gender roles apply when it comes to looking after 'extended families' in a household; there may be family encouragement to focus on academic studies rather than sport Some Muslim woman may choose not to show certain parts of their body or participate in sport with or in front of men	Respect cultural and religious norms and **religious observances** via flexible provision; include single-sex and women-only sessions in provision
Lack of positive sporting role models	A lack of positive sporting role models to encourage participation, which may in part be due to reduced media coverage and a lack of diversity in sports pundits	Promote role models from minority ethnic groups where they exist; employ coaches, commentators and sports pundits from minority ethnic backgrounds
Lack of appropriate activity provision (and awareness of it when it does exist)	Limited provision or lack of appealing activities which meet their needs; a lack of awareness or information about appropriate activity provision (i.e. what is currently available)	Advertise and promote activities specifically targeted to minority ethnic groups; provide appropriate activity options that may appeal to minority ethnic communities
Discrimination or **racism**	Fear of discrimination or racism may discourage people from participating	Enforce anti-discrimination laws and adopt a zero-tolerance policy towards racism and hate speech
Language barriers	People who do not speak the majority language may feel excluded from participating	Produce schedules, signs and advertising materials in different languages; provide translators and interpreters

Cultural norms The rules and expectations of a particular society, based on shared values or traditional beliefs.

Religious observances Behaviour in relation to religious customs (e.g. some religious people may not practise sport on certain days of the week, such as Sunday).

Discrimination The unjust treatment of different categories of people based on characteristics such as ethnicity, sex or disability.

Racism Prejudice, discrimination or antagonism directed against someone of a different race or ethnicity based on the belief that one's own ethnic background is superior.

Exam tip

Make sure you understand the relevant barriers and can specifically link them to the experiences of people from different ethnic groups (e.g. 'a lack of role models for people from minority ethnic groups' rather than just 'a lack of role models').

Typical mistake

When answering questions linked to barriers for people from different ethnic groups, do not include irrelevant answers such as cost or lack of money, lack of time and lack of transport, unless it is suggested in the question, as these barriers can apply to any group.

Check your understanding and progress at www.hoddereducation.co.uk/myrevisionnotes

Retired people or people over the age of 60

Retired people and those who are over the age of 60 may also face barriers to their participation in sport. These barriers are explored in Table 1.6.

Table 1.6 Possible barriers to sport participation for retired people or people over the age of 60, with solutions

Barriers	Example/explanation of barriers	Possible solutions to these barriers
Employment/family commitments	People who are still working full-time may struggle to participate due to lack of time; alternatively, some people may be helping to care for grandchildren, limiting their availability for participation in sport	Provide more flexible programming of sessions for older people, including sessions aimed exclusively at the over 60s
Lack of disposable income	For people who have retired and are no longer earning an income, the costs of participation in sport may become unaffordable – such costs include purchasing equipment, membership or entrance fees and transport costs to sporting venues	Decrease or subsidise the cost of participation or membership
Lack of transport	Older people may struggle with a lack of accessibility to sports clubs, facilities and equipment because they are no longer able to drive or there is no public transport	Provide free transport, arranging lifts to activities or cheaper access to public transport
Lack of positive sporting role models	Some people may be discouraged from participating because of a lack of positive role models aged over 60 to encourage them	Increase positive exposure of professional and amateur sports where people over 60 regularly participate
Lack of appropriate activity provision	There may be limited provision, no suitable sessions or a lack of appealing activities that meet the specific needs of older people	Provide suitable gym machines, and appropriate and appealing activity options for older people (e.g. activities adapted to suit older people's health and fitness levels, as well as activities specifically designed to increase participation among older people, such as recreational walking, bowls and **walking football**)
Lack of awareness of appropriate activity provision	Some older and/or retired people may not be aware of what sporting activities are currently available to them	Advertise and promote activities specifically targeted at retired people and those aged over 60 in venues and places most likely to be accessed by the 60+ age group (e.g. libraries and community centres); offer taster sessions to new participants or for new activities
Lack of mobility or fitness	Some people may struggle with mobility or fitness levels due to long periods of inactivity and/or the increased likelihood of health issues such as osteoporosis, diabetes and high blood pressure; this will negatively impact on their participation	Promote schemes aimed at encouraging participation among older people (e.g. the 'We Are Undefeatable' campaign aimed at the elderly, many of whom have health problems); provide access to medical advice prior to participation and continue to monitor as appropriate via visits to health practitioners

> **Exam tip**
>
> If an exam question asks you to outline or describe barriers to participation for retired people or those over the age of 60, make sure you can expand on each of the examples given above in order to access maximum marks. For example, when explaining lack of time as a potential barrier to over 60s participating in sport, you should mention that people over 60 may still be working and/or spending time looking after their grandchildren.

> **Walking football** This is an adaptation of association football aimed at getting people aged over 50 involved in playing football. The rules have been adapted: they include no running and allow only limited contact.

> **Now test yourself** TESTED ⭕
>
> Visit the Age UK website at www.ageuk.org.uk and search for details of the 'We Are Undefeatable' campaign. Use this information to research and list any barriers to participation in sport for older people, many of whom suffer from health problems, then suggest possible solutions to overcome these barriers.

> **Typical mistake**
>
> When outlining solutions to a lack of participation by retired people or people aged over 60, many students' answers are too brief and not specifically linked to this user group. For example, 'lack of role models' is too vague – instead you need to say 'lack of suitable role models over 60'.

Parents (singles or couples), families with children and people with family commitments

Families with children and/or people with family commitments may also face barriers to their participation in sport. Adults who are also parents may be looking after their children in a couple or be single parents; their individual circumstances will affect the barriers they face.

These barriers are explored in Table 1.7.

Crèche facilities A nursery where young children are cared for (e.g. during a working day or while their parent is participating in a sport or physical activity at a leisure centre).

Table 1.7 Possible barriers to sport participation for people with family commitments and parents, with solutions

Barriers	Example/explanation of barriers	Possible solutions to these barriers
Employment/family commitments	Parents may not have enough free time to participate in sport, due to both childcare and work commitments; some parents may struggle to find suitable activities if their children fall into more than one age group	Plan sessions at times that can accommodate restrictions due to work and school commitments (e.g. mid-morning sessions when older children have been dropped off at school and energy levels are still relatively high; summer holiday activities for the whole family)
Lack of disposable income	Increased expenses for families with children may mean that the costs of participation in sport become unaffordable (e.g. purchasing equipment for children, and membership or entrance fees)	Decrease or subsidise the costs of participation by promoting schemes aimed at families with young children (e.g. family discount membership schemes, holiday clubs)
Lack of positive sporting role models	Lack of sporting role models who discuss their children or families, especially female role models for single mothers	Increase exposure of people involved in sport who have children or family commitments, and how they manage challenges around childcare and other family caring roles
Lack of appropriate activity provision	Lack of activities which the child/children and the parent(s) can enjoy together (particularly if there are large age differences between the children and therefore different interests and needs)	Programming fun activity sessions that the parent(s) and young child/children can join in with (e.g. the Change 4 Life '10 Minute Shake Up' games)
Lack of awareness of appropriate activity provision	Some people may not be aware of suitable sporting activities in their area due to a lack of advertising	Advertise sporting sessions in places that families with children access on a regular basis (e.g. nurseries, schools and play centres)
Lack of childcare provision	Some people may struggle to access sporting activities because there is no childcare provision available for their younger children and/or because of the high costs of childcare	Programme fun activity sessions which both parents and young children can join in with; provide free crèche facilities or access to childcare at sport and leisure facilities
		Providing free **crèche facilities** or access to childcare at sport and leisure centres.

Check your understanding and progress at www.hoddereducation.co.uk/myrevisionnotes

Figure 1.2 A baby swimming class

> **Exam tip**
>
> In an exam question, barriers linked to families and/or family commitments may focus on women or ask you to consider their experiences as part of your answer. This is because women often face additional barriers to participation, despite improvements in access and awareness in recent years.

> **Exam tip**
>
> When answering an exam question about barriers to participation, you must specifically link your answer to the user group identified or described in the question. For example, in the case of barriers faced by single parents, simply stating 'lack of transport' is too vague; lack of transport is a barrier because of cost and so you must make the link clear in order to gain a mark.

> **Typical mistake**
>
> Some students automatically list financial barriers as a reason why families with children do not participate in sport, even when the scenario in the exam question details a family where both parents work (i.e. both adults in the family are earning money, making cost less of a barrier). Remember: not all barriers will apply to every group.

> **Typical mistake**
>
> When writing an answer to an exam question, avoid repeating information that is already provided in the question – this will not gain you any marks.

Carers

Carers may experience a number of barriers to their participation in sport. These barriers are explored in Table 1.8.

Table 1.8 Possible barriers to sport participation for carers, with solutions

Barriers	Example/explanation of barriers	Possible solutions to these barriers
Family commitments	Family commitments may mean carers do not have the time to participate in sport	Provide activities/sessions at various times to meet the needs of different user groups, including carers; provide respite care to free up some time for sporting activities
Lack of disposable income	Carers may not have enough money to access sporting activities (e.g. if they are unable to work due to their carer responsibilities)	Subsidise activities/sessions
Lack of transport	Carers may not have access to suitable transport to travel to sporting facilities	Increase appropriate transport availability if possible (e.g. local buses) or share information about transport networks
Lack of positive family role models or family support	Carers may struggle to participate in sport because of a lack of family role models and/or support	Increase exposure of people involved in sport who have caring responsibilities, and how they manage challenges around time commitments and access

Young children (0–11 years of age)

Young children may experience a number of barriers to their participation in sport. These barriers are explored in Table 1.9.

Table 1.9 Possible barriers to sport participation for young children, with solutions

Barriers	Example/explanation of barriers	Possible solutions to these barriers
Lack of (disposable) income	Young children have no salary and rely on their parents/carers to pay the costs associated with sports participation; if a child's family cannot afford the costs of participation (e.g. transport, equipment, entry fees or lesson costs), participation is unlikely	Decrease or subsidise the costs of participation (e.g. by promoting schemes aimed at encouraging participation among children, providing clubs)
Lack of transport/access	Children may not be able to access sports facilities, perhaps due to their reliance on others for transport or age limits	Community-led group transport; increased networks of parents/carers for sharing of transport
Lack of positive sporting/family role models or family support	Some children may not see positive sporting role models or get parental encouragement to participate	Provide fun and appealing activities to motivate children to participate more; use positive role models children can relate to (e.g. it may help to see their siblings being active); educate parents on the benefits of sport and physical activity for their children
Lack of appropriate activity provision	Poor provision may mean that activities take place at restricted times when children are unable to participate; it may also include limited or unappealing provision in schools	Increase the flexibility of sports provision for children (e.g. adapting equipment and pitch size to suit the age group); improve school provision (e.g. via **school-club links** and taster sessions that give a flavour of an activity; after-school clubs and holiday sport courses; by running gender-specific sessions such as 'girls only' and increasing advertising in schools)
Lack of awareness of appropriate activity provision	Children may not be aware of sporting activities they can participate in	Promote participation opportunities for children via **social media**
Lack of adult supervision	In some sporting sessions, children can only participate if they have adult supervision, such as a parent or guardian	Increase the flexibility of sports provision to enable more parents/carers to attend

Figure 1.3 Young children taking part in a sport class

> **School-club links** An agreement between a school and a community-based sports club to work together to meet the needs of young people.
>
> **Social media** Websites and computer program that allow people to communicate and share information via the internet using a computer, tablet or mobile phone.

Teenagers

Teenagers – individuals of compulsory secondary school age – may experience a number of barriers to their participation in sport. These barriers are explored in Table 1.10.

Table 1.10 Possible barriers to sport participation for teenagers, with solutions

Barriers	Example/explanation of barriers	Possible solutions to these barriers
Lack of disposable income	Some teenagers and their families cannot afford the costs of participation (e.g. transport costs, lesson costs, cost of purchasing equipment, membership or entrance fees)	Decrease or subsidise the costs of participation, or offer concessions
Lack of time	Teenagers may struggle to find time to participate in sport due to other commitments (e.g. as a result of the demands of education, such as exam revision, or, for older teenagers, employment)	Provide more sporting activities held at school or after school
Lack of transport/access	Teenagers may still need to rely on others for transport to sporting facilities	Provide free or subsidised transport to sport facilities
Lack of positive sporting role models or family support	A lack of role models in certain sports may discourage participation, or there may a lack of parental encouragement to participate	Use active, healthy role models to encourage participation (e.g. via schemes such as **Youth Sport Trust Athlete Mentors**) and positive role models that teenagers can relate to; educate parents and teenagers on the benefits of sport and physical activity
Lack of appropriate activity provision	There may be limited PE or sports-club provision (e.g. restricted times when teenagers are able to participate in school, limited PE programmes and/or at local sports clubs)	Improve school provision (e.g. via school-club links or taster sessions that give a flavour of an activity; after-school clubs or holiday sport courses offering appealing activities; increased advertising in schools)
Lack of awareness of appropriate activity provision	Teenagers may not know about the sporting facilities and activities that are available to them	Promote participation opportunities for teenagers via social media
Lack of interest/poor motivation	Some teenagers might not be bothered about sport or feel that studying is more important; other leisure pursuits may be more appealing to them, such as playing computer games or using social media	Promote schemes aimed at encouraging participation among teenagers; increase motivation by promoting the health benefits of activity and providing activities that are fun and appealing to teenagers (e.g. skateboarding, dodgeball)

> **Now test yourself** — TESTED
>
> Draw a 2 × 5 table and write five barriers to participation for teenagers from Table 1.10 in the left-hand column. From memory, try to write appropriate solutions to each barrier in the right-hand column of your table.

> **Exam tip**
>
> An exam question may ask you to write a specific number of points (e.g. 'Identify **three** barriers to participation for teenagers'). Make sure you only give the required number of answers and avoid repeating yourself or making points that are too similar (e.g. avoid stating 'lack of time' as your first point and 'school commitments' as your second).

Youth Sport Trust Athlete Mentors A scheme that involves using some of Britain's most successful athletes to visit schools and inspire young people to get involved in sport – www.youthsporttrust.org

People with disabilities

People with physical, sensory or mental impairments often face extra challenges when trying to participate in sport. These barriers are explored in Table 1.11.

Table 1.11 Possible barriers to sport participation for people with disabilities, with solutions

Barriers	Example/explanation of barriers	Possible solutions to these barriers
Lack of disposable income	There may be high costs for accessible transport and specialist equipment, as well as more general costs relating to membership or entry fees	Subsidise the costs of participation (e.g. offer free swimming for participants and their carers)
Lack of access	Sports facilities may have poor accessibility	Improve access to sporting facilities (e.g. ramps, access doors, hearing loops, disabled parking close to an entrance)
Lack of transport	The availability of adapted or suitable transport may be an issue – not all public transport is accessible and people with certain disabilities may need to be driven or assisted into and out of vehicles	Provide appropriate transport (e.g. a wheelchair-accessible minibus or taxi to and from activity sessions)
Lack of positive sporting role models	People with disabilities may be discouraged from participating due to a lack of visibility of disabled sportspeople or role models and/or a negative portrayal of disabled people in the media	Use role models with disabilities (e.g. Paralympians – Channel 4's 'We're the Superhumans', linked to coverage of the 2016 Summer Paralympics) in advertising campaigns; employ coaches with disabilities to encourage participation
Lack of appropriate activity provision	Sports facilities may have poor provision of adapted or specialist equipment (or difficulty accessing it) – there may also be a lack of specialist facilities that meet the specific needs of people with disabilities; facilities may also lack appealing activities that meet the specific needs of people with disabilities (e.g. those with visual impairment and/or physical impairment)	Provide adapted equipment and facilities (e.g. specialist goal ball for blind or partially sighted people, **hoists** and pool wheelchairs to enable access to swimming pools); provide suitable programmed sessions or adapted activity options (e.g. activities/programmes specifically designed to increase participation among specific groups, such as **Boccia**)
Lack of awareness of appropriate activity provision	People may not be aware of sporting activities due to limited advertising/information about what is currently available for people with disabilities	Advertise or promote activities specifically targeted at people with disabilities and provide information in a variety of accessible formats (e.g. Braille, hearing loops for deaf users)
Lack of confidence	People with disabilities may be discouraged from participating in sport due to a lack of confidence or low self-esteem as a result of concerns and anxieties over access issues or their ability to participate, or due to discrimination or fear of discrimination	Provide separate sessions with specialist coaches to meet the specific needs and varied ability levels of people with disabilities

Hoist A device used to support the lifting and moving of individuals, which enables access to physical activities such as swimming.

Boccia A target sport, involving soft leather balls, that is played indoors by athletes who need high levels of support.

Check your understanding and progress at www.hoddereducation.co.uk/myrevisionnotes

Figure 1.4 Access equipment in a sports context

> **Now test yourself** — TESTED
>
> Consider the solutions to barriers to participation for people with disabilities and make a list of practical examples of how they can be applied (e.g. making physical assistance available to improve access to a facility). Remember: there are many types of disability and not all are visible.

> **Exam tip**
>
> If an exam question asks you to *outline* or explain barriers to participation, do not give a one-word answer. The command words 'outline' and 'explain' mean you should write a detailed answer to fully illustrate your knowledge of the points you are making.

People who work

It is important to be aware that not everyone in society has an unlimited choice of when and where they might participate in physical activity and sport. Those in employment face a number of possible barriers including those explored in Table 1.12.

Table 1.12 Possible barriers to sport participation for people who work, with solutions

Barriers	Example/explanation of barriers	Possible solutions to these barriers
Lack of disposable income	People earning low wages may not have the financial means to cover the cost of participation in sport	Offer appropriate pricing and concessions, reduced membership fees and/or taster sessions for all, including those who work
Lack of appropriate activity provision	People who work may not be able to access sporting facilities during working hours	Offer appropriate activities to appeal to those in work, such as work-based sessions or group activities with like-minded individuals
Lack of awareness of appropriate activity provision	People who work may not know about sporting activities that are available to them	Advertise on social media and use promotional strategies and initiatives which appeal to individuals in employment, such as charity events or sport competitions between different organisations
Lack of free time	People who have long working hours may struggle to find the time to participate in sport	Plan physical activities that will fit in with busy daily lifestyles (e.g. 10-minute HIIT sessions); provide access to facilities and activities at times that will suit people who work

Unemployed/economically disadvantaged people

People who are unemployed, have a low income or are claiming benefits may be less likely to participate in sport. The barriers they face are explored in Table 1.13.

Table 1.13 Possible barriers to sport participation for people who are economically disadvantaged, with solutions

Barriers	Example/explanation of barriers	Possible solutions to these barriers
Lack of disposable income	People who are unemployed or in poorly paid jobs will have little money to spare and so may not prioritise sport or be able to afford the costs involved in participation (e.g. equipment and membership fees)	Promote discounted or free activities (e.g. subsidised classes at leisure centres and participation in free activities such as walking or jogging); subsidise costs associated with participation (e.g. transport and activity costs)
Lack of time	People who need to spend a lot of their available time looking for a job, or who are working in more than one job or working long hours on minimum wage, may struggle to find the time for sport	Provide access to convenient facilities, such as employment advice within sports centres, or workplace activities
Lack of transport	People who do not own cars or who cannot cover the cost of public transport to facilities may be discouraged from participating in sport	Increase local, community-based sport facilities where transport is not needed
Lack of appropriate activity provision	There may be poor availability of activities (e.g. a lack of local clubs, appealing sports or facilities to be active in)	Provide activity options linked to the needs of the unemployed/economically disadvantaged (e.g. specifically designed activities or programmes such as those included in **Street Games** and **Sport for Good**)
Lack of awareness of appropriate activity provision	People may not be aware of activities that are subsidised or provided free of charge	Increase advertising of activities and sports that are available in the local area (e.g. via **Doorstep Sport**)
Lack of motivation	Some people may be experiencing low levels of confidence or self-esteem. This increases the likelihood of adopting unhealthy lifestyle behaviours (e.g. smoking, drinking and eating junk food)	Incentive schemes for healthy activities; medical prescription of physical activity for mental health improvement

Street Games A scheme which uses the power of sport to create positive change in the lives of disadvantaged young people across the UK – www.streetgames.org

Sport for Good A scheme involving sport to tackle three of the features of poverty: youth unemployment, youth crime, and health and wellbeing inequalities.

Doorstep Sport Informal sports clubs that aim to provide a variety of sports to impoverished young people – www.streetgames.org/doorstep-sport

Check your understanding and progress at www.hoddereducation.co.uk/myrevisionnotes

Figure 1.5 Phone fitness apps are useful tools for monitoring fitness and increasing motivation

> **Check your understanding**
>
> 6 How can existing stereotypes act as a barrier to participation for women?
> 7 How can lack of time be overcome as a barrier to young carers?
> 8 People who work often experience a lack of free time due to long working hours. How can this barrier be overcome?

> **Exam tip**
>
> A lack of disposable income or the cost of participation is a common barrier for many different user groups. You can therefore use this barrier as part of your answer to lots of questions, provided your reasons are well explained.

1.4 Factors which can positively and negatively impact upon the popularity of sport in the UK

REVISED

1.4.1 Positive and negative impacts on the popularity of sport in the UK

The number of people participating
+ Sports where there is a strong infrastructure in place are likely to have widespread appeal and mass participation.
+ Increased awareness of the importance of health and fitness has meant lots of fitness clubs are now available, offering activities such as circuit HIIT, spinning, Pilates and yoga.
+ A lot of people participate in a sport like football so it becomes even more popular, unlike fencing which has low numbers of participants and so does not easily increase in popularity.

Topic area 1: The issues which affect participation in sport

The provision of facilities
- Provision includes access to facilities to enable people to watch and participate in sport.
- If sporting facilities such as football/rugby pitches and leisure centres are readily available, it will encourage participation in sport, but if accessibility is more limited (e.g. lack of squash courts), then fewer people will get involved due to limited access.
- The ability to swim is an important life skill, which also helps to develop health and fitness. Swimming can be encouraged via government and local authority investment in good quality provision, i.e. funding local swimming pools throughout the UK or making it part of National Curriculum PE.

Environment/climate activity influences
- Where you live can affect access to some activities (e.g. those living in towns and cities may have limited or no access to coastal areas or large bodies of water for sailing, natural outdoor resources or water sports facilities).
- Travel to access sport and leisure facilities can involve a lengthy journey or high costs, which may negatively impact on participation.
- Even in a shortened 'summer' season, frequent interruptions to play due to bad weather can lead to a loss of interest (e.g. in cricket).
- The lack of mountains or snow limits the availability of activities in some areas of the UK (e.g. snow sports such as skiing and snowboarding are more accessible in Scotland).
- All-weather/5G/6G pitches have improved accessibility to sports like hockey and football even when the weather is poor.

Live spectator opportunities/the amount and range of media coverage
- Watching a sport (in person or on television) or listening to sport on the radio can encourage people to want to take part themselves (e.g. football and rugby get lots of coverage so are popular sports; basketball and handball do not, so see lower participation numbers).
- Watching a favourite team or sporting hero live (e.g. for cyclists, watching the Tour de Yorkshire) can help inspire more people to participate in a sport.
- A lack of opportunity to watch a sport live can negatively impact on participation. For instance, hockey, squash and volleyball are rarely viewed live in large numbers, partly because they receive very little media coverage.
- Media coverage raises the profile of a sport, increasing awareness of it and therefore the likelihood of people choosing to participate in it.
- Free-to-air coverage of a sport and access to it live and on catch-up via a terrestrial TV station or via radio gives access to a far bigger audience than if a sport is only shown on subscription channels such as Sky Sports and BT Sport.
- The Wimbledon tennis championships and the Olympic Games are televised on the BBC in the UK as a free-to-air channel, while cricket (e.g. the Ashes) is currently only available to watch via Sky Sports, which is a subscription-based channel. The rights to broadcast the UEFA Champions League football coverage are held by BT Sport.
- Some argue that broadcasting sports on anything other than free-to-air television is negative as it automatically limits access to the sport, especially to certain groups.

> **Terrestrial TV stations**
> Free-to-air TV, such as BBC, ITV, Channel 4 and Channel 5 in the UK.
>
> **Sky Sports** The main subscription-based sports channel provider in the UK.

- However, it can also be said that Sky Sports has had a positive influence on the coverage of sports such as netball, which receive limited coverage on terrestrial TV. This may positively influence opportunities to participate in a sport at the elite level.
- Increased media coverage of a sport generates more income via sponsorship opportunities and media rights, which can then be invested into providing further opportunities to participate in the sport. For example, the English and Wales Cricket Board (ECB), which is the governing body of cricket in England and Wales, invests income from media coverage into the management and development of all forms of cricket for both male and female participants, from junior levels up to international standard.

The high-level success for both individuals and teams
- When a team is successful at a major sporting event, it can inspire and encourage participation in that sport. For example, the England netball team won gold at the Commonwealth Games in 2018, while the England cricket team won the World Cup in 2019 in a game which finished with a tie-break 'super over'. This has resulted in more people becoming interested in these sports. Conversely, if success is lacking, a sport will not be as popular (e.g. basketball, handball and ice hockey).
- Individual success can also serve as a source of inspiration for people to aspire to. Emma Raducanu winning the US Open in 2021 will likely inspire more people to take up tennis.

The number and range of positive role models available in a sport
- Having lots of positive role models to aspire to can encourage people to take up sport, while a lack of them can be a negative factor that means people are less likely to participate.
- The lack of positive role models to aspire to is seen as a common cause of lower participation rates for particular user groups, such as the relative lack of British Asian football players or high-profile females in sports such as cricket and rugby.

Social acceptability
- Some sports have a particular culture that negatively influences participation in that sport. For instance, boxing has been criticised for being violent and causing injury (e.g. to the head) to the participants during the normal course of competition, as the sport involves punching an opponent.
- Dance is seen by many as a feminine 'aesthetic' sport and as more acceptable and popular with girls than boys.

> **Exam tip**
>
> To score more marks, you will need to know and be able to link various factors influencing the popularity of a sport in the UK to relevant sporting examples in order to illustrate the point you are making.

> **Typical mistake**
>
> If an exam question asks you to 'evaluate' or 'discuss' the impact of factors affecting participation in sports, remember to include both negative and positive points. If you only give one set of points (i.e. negative or positive), you will limit the marks available to you.

> **Check your understanding**
>
> 9 Why might climate be a negative influence on the popularity of cricket in the UK?
> 10 What is a positive impact on the popularity of sport of showing sport on terrestrial TV rather than satellite channels?
> 11 Why is boxing a socially 'unacceptable' sport?

1.5 Emerging/new sports in the UK

1.5.1 The growth of emerging/new sports in the UK

New and emerging sports and activities are becoming more popular and seeking to establish themselves in the UK. Some examples of current emerging sports include:

- Ultimate Frisbee
- footgolf
- korfball
- handball
- futsal
- padel tennis
- parkour.

> **Korfball** A ball sport with similarities to netball and basketball played by two teams of eight players (four male and four female), with the aim of throwing the ball into a net.
>
> **Futsal** A variation on association football (soccer) played on a hard court with a smaller, low-bounce ball.

Opportunities to develop and participate in emerging sports can be increased by:

- encouraging more people to do it
- providing suitable facilities, pitches and/or equipment
- providing more competitions
- training more coaches and officials
- increasing the number of clubs available to join
- increasing media coverage and using role models to encourage participation
- advertising and promotion
- offering taster sessions or subsidised coaching sessions
- adapting the sport for different user groups (e.g. non-contact)
- offering the sport in school PE programmes (e.g. either as part of the curriculum, as part of an examined course, such as Futsal in GCSE/A level PE, or as an extra-curricular activity)
- organising grassroots schemes to encourage participation in physical activity at the lowest, most local level for health, educational or social purposes.

Futsal is an example of an emerging sport in the UK. Some of the reasons why it is increasing in popularity include the fact that:

- it can be played indoors, so can be played all year round, and indoor facilities can be adapted quite easily to suit play
- it is accessible to different levels, ages and abilities, as it is easier to play and has more involvement than 11-a-side association football
- it is useful in developing skills for association football
- matches are shorter, so it can be played in reduced time-periods, which suits the lifestyle of some participants (e.g. working people)
- more competitive opportunities are becoming available; there is now greater promotion of futsal.

Figure 1.6 Futsal is an emerging sport in the UK

Check your understanding and progress at www.hoddereducation.co.uk/myrevisionnotes

Figure 1.7 Padel tennis

Padel tennis is an example of an emerging sport that may also help to increase interest in playing tennis. It is a mix of tennis and squash played on a court approximately half the size of a traditional tennis court, with a walled edge and using modified equipment. Padel tennis can be played indoors or outdoors.

The following factors may explain its popularity:
+ It is easy to play as the ball strike is close to the hand/body.
+ It is rewarding to learn as players' skills can accelerate rapidly.
+ It is very sociable as it is always played in doubles.
+ It can be played by people with varying fitness levels.
+ It can be flexible in terms of time and space.

> **Now test yourself** TESTED
>
> Identify an emerging sport that is available to participate in close to where you live (e.g. futsal or footgolf). Investigate how this sport is trying to attract more people to play. Make bullet point notes of your main findings.

> **Exam tip**
>
> To score more marks, be prepared to outline different ways in which an emerging sport can be developed and opportunities to participate be increased in the UK.

> **Check your understanding**
>
> 12 Identify three sports which are sometimes incorrectly used as examples of emerging sports in the UK.
> 13 Why might futsal be a good activity for busy working people to play?

> **Typical mistake**
>
> When describing emerging sports, do not give an incorrect example; for instance, netball, basketball, swimming, rounders and athletics are all established sports and would not gain any marks.

> **Exam checklist**
>
> In this section you learned about issues which affect participation in sport, including:
> + different user groups who participate in sport
> + possible barriers affecting participation in sport
> + possible solutions to the barriers affecting participation in sport
> + how to apply barriers to participation and possible solutions to these barriers to different user groups
> + factors which can positively and negatively impact on the popularity of sport in the UK
> + the growth of emerging/new sports in the UK.

Topic area 1: The issues which affect participation in sport

Exam-style questions

1. Jane is a single parent with two young children. She is currently unemployed. Jane is keen to try a new sport.
   a. Identify three barriers that might prevent Jane from taking part regularly in sport. [3]
   b. Suggest an emerging sport that Jane could participate in. [1]

2. A local sports centre is trying to increase the participation in physical activity of people with disabilities.
   a. Identify four barriers that can prevent people with disabilities from participating at their local sports centre. [4]
   b. Describe two ways the centre could make it easier for people with physical disabilities to take part in swimming, and give an example for each. [4]

3. One barrier to teenagers participating in sport is a lack of money. Give *two other barriers* that might prevent teenagers from participating in sport, and suggest a possible solution to each barrier. [4]

4. Participation in recreational swimming tends to increase after major events such as the Olympics, partly due to the increased media coverage it receives.
   Apart from media coverage, describe two factors which impact on the popularity of swimming in the UK. [4]

5. Mio is a 16-year-old teenage girl who is studying for her end-of-year examinations but would like to participate in more sport.
   a. Identify three barriers that might prevent Mio from regular participation in sport. [3]
   b. Suggest two solutions that could help Mio to participate in more sport. [2]

6. A local tennis club would like to encourage more people over the age of 60 to play tennis.
   a. Explain how the following barriers may prevent people over the age of 60 from playing tennis.
      i. Cost [1]
      ii. Provision [1]
   b. For each of the following, give one solution the tennis club could use to promote tennis to people over the age of 60.
      i. Cost [1]
      ii. Provision [1]

7. Alya tells her friends that she wants to go to a weekly exercise class with them but keeps finding excuses not to. Alya is 40 years old and lives in a central Manchester flat. She has a 9 to 5 job and is a single parent with a 6-year-old son.
   Using the information above, identify four user groups which apply to Alya. [4]

8. A local sports centre introduces a new exercise class at 11 a.m. from Monday to Friday.
   a. Identify two user groups who are likely to be able to participate in this class. [2]
   b. Identify two user groups who are unlikely to be able to participate in this class. [2]

9. Which of the following *is* a user group experiencing limited access to sport? [1]
   a. People who are healthy
   b. People who are unemployed
   c. People who are able bodied
   d. People who are economically secure

10. Using examples, explain two reasons why the 'climate' can have a negative impact on the popularity of a sport in the UK. [2]

11. Apart from media coverage, describe a factor which can affect the popularity of each type of sport given below:
    a. Winter sports (e.g. snowboarding) [1]
    b. Martial arts (e.g. taekwondo) [1]

12. Which of the following is an example of an emerging sport in the UK? [1]
    a. Netball
    b. Korfball
    c. Basketball
    d. Rugby football

13. Identify four factors which can affect the growth of an emerging sport in the UK. [4]

14. Footgolf is an example of an emerging sport in the UK. Give two potential barriers to participation in an emerging sport. [2]

15. Explain the factors affecting the popularity of different sports in the UK. [8]

Topic area 2: The role of sport in promoting values

2.1 Sport values

REVISED

2.1.1 Values which can be promoted through sport

There are a number of **values** that can be encouraged through sport, such as those identified and explained in Table 2.1.

> **Values** The principles which help you decide what is right and what is wrong.

Table 2.1 Values that can be promoted through sport

Value	Explanation	Example
Team spirit	Where you learn how to work together; refers to the support given to a fellow team or squad member, and the ability to work together to reach a collective goal	In sporting events such as the Davis Cup in tennis, team members can get a feeling of pride and loyalty that motivates them to support each other and work hard to do their best for the team, and ultimately improve their chances of success
Fair play	Where performers adhere to the rules and do not cheat while performing, and show highly appropriate, polite behaviour; this includes respecting opponents and being fair to others	Maintaining silence when a rugby player is about to take a conversion or a golfer is about to play a shot
Citizenship	Relates to how people create community links and community spirit by getting involved in local clubs and teams; sport provides people with a chance to act as 'good citizens' by getting involved in their local community	People acting as volunteers or sports coaches, helping to run local community sports clubs
Tolerance AND respect	Seen as one sporting value, not two separate values; sport is a good way of developing an understanding of different countries and their cultures	Events such as the Commonwealth Games are used to promote mutual tolerance and respect among opponents, including showing respect for other countries' national anthems when played at medal ceremonies
Inclusion	Refers to the fact that in order for all social groups to participate in sport, there should be equal opportunities for all groups in society to play sport; **social inclusion** involves the use of sport, via a variety of schemes/initiatives, to get under-represented social groups involved in sport	'This Girl Can' was a Sport England-led campaign to get more women involved in sport as an under-represented social group
National pride	Support for your national team or squad in a sport, created by uniting the whole population in their support; international sporting events are a good way of promoting this sense of unity in performers and spectators – it can involve wearing team kit and/or congregating in city centres at open-air events to support the national team	England cricket and England netball in their respective World Cup competitions in 2019; large gatherings to support the national football team at the Euros or the FIFA World Cup
Excellence	Involves encouraging sports performers to strive to develop themselves to the full and to achieve excellence in their favourite sport via consistent, top-level performance	

Figure 2.1 Participants in international sporting events often sing their national anthem

> **Tolerance AND respect** Accepting and welcoming players from different social backgrounds.
>
> **Social inclusion** Making sure all community groups have an opportunity to participate in sport.
>
> **Excellence** When performers strive to be the very best they can in their chosen activity and work with maximum effort.

Exam tip

To earn as many marks as possible, you need to be able to use relevant examples of each value applied in a sporting context.

Now test yourself TESTED

Reflecting on your own sporting experience/involvement, consider how the value of 'excellence' is being promoted in you.

Typical mistake

When asked to give sporting examples linked to citizenship, some people incorrectly refer to unity in the population (i.e. national pride) rather than the creation of community links and community spirit through sporting involvement such as volunteering at a local sports club.

Check your understanding

1. Identify seven values which can be promoted through sport.
2. Give an example of citizenship applied in a sporting context.
3. Summarise what is meant by tolerance and respect as a sporting value.

2.2 The Olympic and Paralympic movement

2.2.1 Olympic and Paralympic

The Olympic and Paralympic movement has a number of important principles you need to know, including the creed, the symbol and the Olympic and Paralympic values:

+ **The Olympic Creed:** This is a moral message or statement outlining the value of endeavour and trying your best to overcome challenges. It was written at the end of the nineteenth century by Baron Pierre de Coubertin and first spoken in 1908, and reads as follows: 'The most important thing is not to win but to take part, just as the most important thing in life is not the triumph but the struggle. The essential thing is not to have conquered, but to have fought well.'
+ **The Olympic Symbol:** This is the five interlocking rings that represent the closeness/union of all five continents of the world that take part in the Olympics.
+ **The Olympic and Paralympic values**: These are a number of different values as stated and defined/linked to sporting examples in Tables 2.2 and 2.3.

Check your understanding and progress at www.hoddereducation.co.uk/myrevisionnotes

Table 2.2 The Olympic values as defined by the International Olympic Committee (IOC)

Value	Definition/link to sporting examples
Excellence	Someone doing the best they can, in sport and in life. It is about taking part and striving for improvement, not just winning (e.g. achieving a personal best), making progress and enjoying the healthy combination of body, will and mind
Friendship	This is the heart of the Olympic Movement – using sport to develop tolerance and mutual understanding between all people, performers, spectators and citizens generally (e.g. athletes from different nations making friends with athletes from other countries at the closing ceremony)
Respect	Having consideration for yourself and your body, others and the wider environment; it includes respecting the rules and regulations of sport and the officials who uphold them (e.g. shaking hands with officials and congratulating an opponent at the end of an event; applauding and/or congratulating opponents at the end of a competition; treating people with disabilities with dignity)

Table 2.3 The Paralympic values

Value	Definition/link to sporting examples
Inspiration	Paralympic athletes maximise their abilities, empowering and inspiring others to be active and to participate in sport (i.e. acting as positive role models to follow)
Determination	Paralympic athletes have a unique strength of character that combines mental toughness, physical ability and outstanding agility to produce sporting performances that regularly redefine the boundaries of possibility and overcome any barriers to training and competing (e.g. lack of self-belief)
Courage	Paralympic athletes showcase to the world what can be achieved when testing your body to its absolute limits (e.g. overcoming an injury to train hard and compete at an event)
Equality	Paralympic athletes celebrate diversity and show that difference is a strength; they champion equal rights (e.g. gender, race or disability) and challenge stereotypes about and discrimination towards people with disabilities

> **Exam tip**
>
> Ensure you make the appropriate number of comments/answers according to the marks available for a question (i.e. remember LAMA – Look At Mark Allocation!).
>
> To score more marks, you can use mnemonics to help you remember key words (e.g. '**REF**' as a way of remembering the Olympic values of **R**espect, **E**xcellence and **F**riendship; '**DICE**' as a way of remembering the Paralympic values of **D**etermination, **I**nspiration, **C**ourage and **E**quality).

> **Now test yourself** TESTED
>
> Reinforce your knowledge and understanding of this topic area by viewing YouTube/internet clips on 'the Olympic Creed' and 'the Olympic and Paralympic values'. Watch the clips:
> + Olympic Creed: https://www.youtube.com/watch?v=BR8ZbNmIyNw
> + Paralympic values: https://www.youtube.com/watch?v=sOXbQLLTwVQ
> + Olympic values: https://www.youtube.com/watch?v=Vy9a-z946Rg

> **Check your understanding**
>
> 4 What does the Olympic symbol represent?
> 5 Identify the three Olympic values.
> 6 List the four Paralympic values.
> 7 How does the Olympic Creed link to the Paralympic value of 'determination'?

> **Typical mistake**
>
> Do not incorrectly mix up your understanding of sporting values you have previously learned about (e.g. national pride and team spirit) with the three Olympic and four Paralympic values.

2.3 Sporting values, initiatives and campaigns

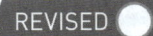

2.3.1 Other initiatives, campaigns and events which promote sporting values

There are a range of initiatives, campaigns and events which promote values through sport – these can be local, regional or national.

Sports initiatives and events or campaigns can be used to promote certain values in those taking part, as outlined in Table 2.4.

Table 2.4 Sports initiatives and the values they promote

Sports initiatives/campaigns	Values promoted
Sport Relief	**Citizenship/tolerance and respect:** Sport Relief is a charity event from Comic Relief, in association with BBC Sport, which brings together the worlds of sport and entertainment to raise money to help vulnerable people in both the UK and the world's poorest countries. This fundraising campaign therefore encourages people to get active and to raise money for vulnerable people in the UK and abroad. In 2020, this saw eight celebrities complete a 100-mile expedition across the Namib desert.
The ECB's 'Chance to Shine' campaign (e.g. 'Chance to Shine Street')	**Team spirit/inclusion:** A scheme aimed at trying to ensure that cricket continues to be played in state schools and inner-city areas where it is particularly under threat and children may not have been given the chance to play it. The ECB's partnership with 'Chance to Shine' links in with Cricket Unleashed, a new framework for cricket in England and Wales. Cricket Unleashed commits the sport to inspire more people and families to play and follow cricket, and to take the game into new places and communities.
FIFA's 'Football for Hope' campaign	**Inclusion:** A collaboration between FIFA and 'Street Football World', this programme is a social project for disadvantaged people, using football as a focal and unifying point.
Sport England's 'This Girl Can' campaign	**Inclusion:** A scheme aimed at breaking down barriers to participation for women (e.g. lack of confidence or fear of judgement).
The FA's 'Respect' campaign	**Fair play/tolerance and respect:** This campaign encourages appropriate behaviour between footballers and in particular towards officials during matches. The new FA campaign 'We Only Do Positive' is targeting coaches and parents within mini-soccer and youth football. 'We Only Do Positive' aims to promote and educate coaches and parents on their roles in creating a fun, safe and inclusive environment for all the players, ensuring they have great experiences throughout their football journey.
Kick it Out	**Inclusion/tolerance and respect:** Kick it Out are an organisation working hard to promote inclusion and equality in sports and to decrease racism. A small independent charity, the 'Let's Kick Racism Out of Football' campaign was established in 1993 in response to widespread calls from clubs, players and fans to tackle racist attitudes existing within the game. Kick It Out was then established as a body in 1997, widening its objectives to cover all aspects of discrimination, inequality and exclusion.
Sporting Equals	**Inclusion and citizenship:** Sporting Equals' aim is to promote ethnic diversity across sport and physical activity. They want to see more black and minority ethnic communities being involved in sport as participants, volunteers or coaches.
Rainbow Laces (LGBTQ+)	**Inclusion:** Rainbow Laces is a Stonewall campaign in which participants do something active while wearing rainbow laces in their boots or trainers, to show their support for LGBTQ+ equality.

Check your understanding and progress at www.hoddereducation.co.uk/myrevisionnotes

Figure 2.2 Wearing rainbow laces to show support for LGBTQ+ equality

Chance to Shine A national charity that aims to give all children the opportunity to play, learn and develop through cricket (e.g. through 'Chance to Shine Schools' and 'Chance to Shine Street').

Chance to Shine Street A scheme which gives children and young adults in inner-city areas the opportunity to play cricket. It is played with a tapeball (a tennis ball wrapped in electrical tape) and plastic bats, and matches last for just 20 minutes – it's cricket's answer to five-a-side football!

FA 'Respect' The FA's 'Respect' programme was launched in the 2008–09 season following a build-up of behavioural problems in the National Game.

Kick It Out English football's equality and inclusion organisation, it works throughout the football, educational and community sectors to challenge discrimination, encourage inclusive practices and campaign for positive change. Kick It Out is at the heart of the fight against discrimination for everyone who plays, watches or works in football.

> **Exam tip**
> To earn more marks, make sure you can link appropriate sporting values to different sporting initiatives and/or campaigns.

> **Now test yourself** — TESTED
> Reinforce your knowledge and understanding of this topic area by doing research on the internet to find a local sporting initiative, campaign or event. Try to link this initiative to its role in promoting sports values (see section 2.1 for examples of sports values to refer to as you do your research).

> **Check your understanding**
> 8 How does Kick it Out seek to promote the value of inclusion in sport?
> 9 Identify two other initiatives or campaigns which also promote the value of inclusion.

> **Typical mistake**
> Be careful not to incorrectly link initiatives or campaigns to the sporting values they promote or to use the incorrect terms/names when giving examples of initiatives or campaigns promoting sporting values.

2.4 The importance of etiquette AND sporting behaviour

REVISED

2.4.1 The importance of etiquette AND sporting behaviour of performers

Sports played with a high level of etiquette are often admired by spectators. This is due to the positive sporting behaviour observed (e.g. polite and mutually respectful fair play).

The reasons for observing etiquette and sporting behaviour

There are a variety of reasons why performers should observe etiquette and positive sporting behaviour (e.g. sportsmanship), such as:

+ ensuring fairness/that a fair result is achieved
+ promoting and reinforcing positive values (e.g. respect for others)
+ helping to ensure the safety of themselves and their opponents
+ setting a good example to young people and providing a positive role model to children
+ improving the reputation of the sport and encouraging participation in the sport
+ ensuring an activity/game can be played effectively in a free-flowing/enjoyable manner
+ possibly gaining sponsorship deals for an elite/professional performer.

Sportsmanship

Sportsmanship involves adhering to the written rules of sport and playing within the letter and the spirit of the sport. It also involves the unwritten codes of conduct, as illustrated by the examples below:

+ applauding the performance or success of an opponent (e.g. playing an inventive shot in tennis; scoring a goal in netball)
+ shaking hands with opponents and officials before and/or after a game; boxers touching gloves before the start of the last round
+ showing grace and respect at the end of a game whether you have won or lost
+ showing respect to and freely accepting the decisions of officials
+ returning the ball to the opposition in football when they have kicked it out because of an injury to one of your team
+ 'walking' in cricket when you know you are out (e.g. you have edged the ball through to the wicket keeper)
+ being honest in badminton or tennis by signalling a foot fault on service or making an honest call on a close ball 'in or out' decision.

Gamesmanship

With ever-increasing rewards for winning at stake, some sports performers resort to negative sporting behaviour via their use of gamesmanship to gain an advantage over their opponents. Examples of gamesmanship include:

+ delaying a restart to a contest or 'running down the clock' (i.e. wasting time) when winning
+ over-appealing (i.e. excessive complaining, e.g. in cricket to pressure an umpire into making a decision to benefit your team)
+ taking time out for an injury even when you are not injured (e.g. in cricket or tennis)
+ grunting loudly in tennis when playing a shot in order to put an opponent off.

It is important to encourage and reinforce sportsmanship when participating in sport rather than using gamesmanship to bend the rules in order to be successful.

> **Typical mistake**
>
> Be careful not to incorrectly define gamesmanship as 'fair play'.

2.4.2 The importance of etiquette AND sporting behaviour of spectators

In addition to performers showing etiquette during sporting contests, spectators of such events also need to behave appropriately. Examples of spectator etiquette include:

+ being quiet during play (e.g. as a tennis player is about to serve at Wimbledon, or a golfer is about to putt at The Open Championship, or a snooker player is about to take a shot)
+ remaining quiet and standing up while an opposition's national anthem plays in order to show tolerance and respect of different countries through sport
+ respecting and accepting decisions made by officials and not swearing or using aggressive behaviour towards them
+ not making negative comments or directing racist/sexist chants towards other players, supporters or officials
+ not going onto the playing area (e.g. respecting the line in football via 'non-trespass')
+ not displaying aggressive behaviour (e.g. towards officials or the opposition)
+ recognising good performance from both teams (e.g. applauding an opponent's skill or goal)
+ observing the safety of players (e.g. not throwing items onto the pitch during a football match).

It is important to note that spectators have a responsibility to view the sporting action in a manner that does not jeopardise their fellow spectators or the players.

> **Etiquette** The unwritten rules concerning player behaviour.
>
> **Gamesmanship** Bending the rules and/or stretching them to their absolute limit in order to gain an advantage in sport.
>
> **Spectator etiquette** The rules or guidelines for spectators at a sporting event.

> **Exam tip**
>
> To earn more marks, make sure you can give practical examples of etiquette and/or sporting behaviour for both performers and spectators.

> **Typical mistake**
>
> Avoid giving irrelevant examples of sporting etiquette. For example, helping an opponent up off the floor when you have fouled them misses the point about what sportsmanship is, because it was poor etiquette to commit the foul in the first place.

Now test yourself
TESTED

Reinforce your knowledge of this topic area by choosing a sporting activity (e.g. tennis, football or cricket) and identifying two examples of sportsmanship, gamesmanship and spectator etiquette in your chosen sport in order to complete the revision table below:

Sporting activity:	
Examples of sportsmanship	1.
	2.
Examples of gamesmanship	1.
	2.
Examples of spectator etiquette	1.
	2.

Check your understanding

10 Define 'etiquette'.
11 Define 'spectator etiquette'.
12 Identify the reasons why observing etiquette is important for a sports performer.
13 Identify three sporting examples of times when spectators are expected to maintain their silence.
14 Identify whether the following are examples of sportsmanship or gamesmanship:
   a Time wasting
   b Shaking hands with opponents at the end of a game
   c Over-appealing
   d Taking an unnecessary injury time out (e.g. in tennis)
   e Sledging/saying things to put an opponent off
15 Give an example from golf of a time when both participants and spectators would be expected to observe 'appropriate etiquette'.

2.5 The use of Performance Enhancing Drugs (PEDs) in sport

2.5.1 The reasons why sports performers use PEDs

Sports performers may choose to use prohibited PEDs for a number of different reasons, including:
+ pressure to win or to succeed as an individual
+ pressure from the media or nation to win
+ pressure from coaches to take them in order to increase their chances of winning
+ to gain money or fame as a result of success
+ to improve performance (e.g. via improved fitness, strength, stamina or power)
+ to improve recovery time (e.g. from training or from injury)
+ to increase the ability to train (i.e. for longer or harder)
+ to mask (i.e. cover up) pain
+ to lose weight
+ to level the playing field because of the belief that others are taking PEDs.

2.5.2 The reasons why performers should not use PEDs

There are a number of reasons why PEDs should not be used, including the following:
+ they can lead to long-term ill health (both physical and/or mental), addiction or over-reliance on PEDs
+ there are sanctions (i.e. negative consequences) when found guilty (e.g. long-term bans, fines or financial penalties such as the loss of prize money, and the potential loss of sponsorship)
+ they give an unfair advantage against 'clean athletes' who have not taken PEDs
+ PED use is cheating/against the rules
+ they are detrimental to the sport and give it a bad name (e.g. cycling or athletics where there is a mistrust of results)
+ it can reflect badly on an individual or nation.

2.5.3 The role of the World Anti-Doping Agency (WADA) in eradicating the use of PEDs

The World Anti-Doping Agency (WADA) is an organisation that aims to ensure a drug-free sporting environment across the world. Its main activities include scientific research, education, the development of anti-doping methods and monitoring of the World Anti-Doping Code.

WADA's Whereabouts Rule

This important strategy aims to ensure the drug-free sporting environment WADA is aiming for. It involves a select group of named elite athletes who provide information to the 'authorities' (e.g. the UK Anti-Doping Agency [UKAD]). Athletes must:
+ provide information about their location (outside of competition)
+ be available for a 60-minute timeslot in an agreed place every day
+ understand that three missed tests in a year results in a sanction.

WADA testing methods

WADA uses a number of testing methods to try to catch out athletes who are using illegal PEDs. These include:
+ blood sample collection
+ urine sample collection

World Anti-Doping Agency (WADA) A foundation initiated by the International Olympic Committee based in Canada to promote, coordinate and monitor the fight against drugs in sports.

World Anti-Doping Code The World Anti-Doping Code is the core document that harmonises (i.e. tries to make the same) anti-doping policies, rules and regulations within sport organisations and among public authorities around the world.

UK Anti-Doping Agency (UKAD) The national anti-doping organisation in the UK.

- hair sample collection
- nail sample collection.

2.5.4 Sanctions to prevent the use of PEDs

The battle against illegal PEDs is continuous and involves a variety of different initiatives and strategies in an attempt to make sport drug-free. Examples of such initiatives and strategies include:
- the creation of partnerships (i.e. cross-organisation work between WADA and National Anti-Doping Organisations [NADOs])
- random drugs testing/WADA's Whereabouts Rule
- harsher punishments for those found guilty of taking illegal PEDs (e.g. long-term bans and/or fines)
- the loss of sponsorship or National Lottery funding for those found guilty of taking PEDs
- the loss of medals or the deletion of records.

2.5.5 Educational strategies to prevent the use of PEDs

Educational strategies to discourage the use of PEDs often involve the use of campaigns led by role models, peers and family members. These campaigns focus on the (health) risks of taking PEDs and the importance of creating an ethically fair and drug-free approach to competing (e.g. via '100% Me', which uses positive sporting role models to promote its message of drug-free sport and achievement through hard work and dedication in order to develop talents to the full).

> **100% Me** The UKAD's education and information programme to help athletes retain an ethically fair, drug-free approach to sport.

2.5.6 Impact of the use of PEDs on the sport

As well as affecting the reputation of an individual athlete, PED scandals can have a wider impact on the sport:
- The sport may gain a negative reputation or image (e.g. cycling or weightlifting).
- The sport may see a reduction in income or sponsorship.
- Mistrust of results; spectators may question whether they are watching 'clean' and fair sport.
- Spectators may mistrust events following large numbers of positive tests or scandals (e.g. among 100 m Olympic sprinters and Tour de France cyclists).
- There may be scepticism about all performers in a sport if there are lots of PED cases in that sport.
- Young people may be put off taking up the sport and it could suffer from decreased participation.

> **Exam tip**
>
> To earn more marks, make sure that when extended questions are set, you develop the points you make and link them to relevant examples. It is also important to reach a justified conclusion when a question requires it.

> **Now test yourself** TESTED
>
> Research WADA (e.g. via a YouTube clip) and note down any points on how WADA is working to try and eradicate the use of PEDs in sport.

> **Typical mistake**
>
> Students often lose marks by not answering the question that is given. For example, if a question focuses on the impact of PEDs on the *career* of an athlete, do not give answers linked to the athlete's health as these would be irrelevant and gain no marks.

> **Check your understanding**
>
> 16 What do the initials 'WADA' stand for?
> 17 What is the name of the organisation responsible for drug prevention and detection in the UK?

Topic area 2: The role of sport in promoting values

Exam checklist

In this section you learned about the role of sport in promoting values. These values were explored in a range of topic areas, including:
+ the values which can be promoted through sport
+ examples of each value in a sporting context
+ the Olympic and Paralympic movement and the values it promotes
+ how sporting initiatives, campaigns and events are used to promote sporting values
+ the importance of etiquette AND sporting behaviour of performers
+ the importance of etiquette AND sporting behaviour of spectators
+ the use of Performance Enhancing Drugs (PEDs) in sport
+ the reasons why sports performers use drugs and the reasons why they should not
+ the role of the World Anti-Doping Agency (WADA) in eradicating the use of PEDs
+ sanctions and educational strategies to prevent the use of PEDs
+ the impact of the use of PEDs on sport.

Exam-style questions

1 Identify whether the following three statements are true or false.
   The *Olympic Creed* states that:
   a winning is more important than taking part [1]
   b it is important to have fought well in sports competition [1]
   c the struggle to achieve your best is more important than the triumph. [1]

2 Identify which three of the following are *not* Olympic values. [3]
   Excellence National pride Citizenship Respect Friendship Inclusion

3 State three values associated with the Paralympics. [3]

4 Draw a line to match each of the following sporting values to the correct example. [3]

Sporting value		Example	
1	Citizenship	a	Supporters uniting behind Team GB at the Olympics/Paralympics
2	National pride	b	Making sure all user groups (e.g. minority ethnic groups or people with disabilities) are given the opportunity to participate in sport
3	Inclusion	c	Volunteering to coach your local U-10 netball team

5 Identify three ways that a young footballer can show good sportsmanship. [3]

6 State two reasons why it is important to maintain the ethic of sportsmanship in modern-day sport. [2]

7 Which of the following is not an example of gamesmanship? [1]
   a Wasting time when winning 1–0 towards the end of a game
   b Taking an injury time-out during a tennis match, even when fully fit
   c Over-appealing to the umpire in a cricket match
   d Shaking hands with your opponents at the end of a football match

8 Outline three practical sporting examples of gamesmanship. [3]

9 Explain three examples of spectator etiquette during a sporting contest. [3]

10 Identify three reasons why some sports performers may use Performance Enhancing Drugs (PEDs). [3]

11 Identify three reasons why sports performers should not use PEDs. [3]

12 Describe WADA's Whereabouts Rule used in testing for the use of PEDs. [2]

13 Describe two negative impacts for a sport of athletes taking PEDs. [2]

14 State two ways to prevent illegal drug use in sport. [2]

15 Identify a sports initiative and a value it promotes. [2]

16 Draw a line to link each sports initiative to the relevant sporting values it promotes. [3]

Sports initiative		Sporting values	
1	FA's 'Respect' campaign	a	Team spirit/inclusion
2	Chance to Shine	b	Fair play/tolerance and respect
3	Sport Relief	c	Citizenship/tolerance and respect

17 Explain the benefits of the Olympic and Paralympic values and positive sporting behaviour at major sporting events such as the Olympics and Paralympics. [8]

Check your understanding and progress at www.hoddereducation.co.uk/myrevisionnotes

Topic area 3: The implications of hosting a major sporting event for a city or country

3.1 The features of a major sporting event

REVISED

3.1.1 The types and scheduling of major sporting events

Major sporting events require a lot of organisation; some take a very long time to put together to ensure the smooth running of the event for all concerned (e.g. performers, coaches, media and fans). These events therefore take place according to a set schedule at certain times.

Major sporting events frequently occur all across the world. This section of the syllabus requires knowledge and understanding of how such events are organised and scheduled in three different ways: regular, 'one-off', and regular and recurring.

Regular events
Regular events are very important sporting occasions that are held in a different city each year, but could return to the same venue after a few years. Examples of regular sporting events include the:
- UEFA Champions League Final and the Europa League Final, which are hosted by different cities selected by UEFA from around Europe
- Diamond League Athletics Final
- British Open Golf Championships.

One-off events
One-off events are held once at a particular time with a host city staging the sporting competition once in a generation. Examples of one-off events include:
- multi-sport competitions such as the Asian games, the Olympics, the Paralympics and the Commonwealth Games
- single-sport competitions for men and women such as the FIFA World Cup (football) and World Cups in cricket, rugby league and rugby union.

Regular and recurring events
Many sporting events are regular and recurring, which means that they are held annually (i.e. each year) at the same venue or host city. Examples of such events include the:
- Formula 1 Grand Prix races (e.g. Formula 1 British Grand Prix at Silverstone)
- Wimbledon Tennis Championships held annually at the All England Lawn Tennis and Croquet Club in London
- FA Cup Finals for men and women held at Wembley Stadium
- London Marathon and Great North Run held in London and north-east England respectively
- World Snooker Championships held at the Crucible Theatre in Sheffield.

> **Regular** Held in a different city each year but could return to a previous location after a few years.
>
> **One-off** Held in a host city once in a generation.
>
> **Regular and recurring** Held each year at the same venue or city.

> **Exam tip**
>
> To clarify your knowledge and understanding of the different types and scheduling of major sporting events, you must be able to apply it to named sporting examples across different types of sporting activities.

> **Exam tip**
>
> To ensure you earn marks when asked for examples of regular events, make sure you use the word 'Final' where there are several stages or rounds to a competition (e.g. the FA Final; the UEFA Champions League Final).

Figure 3.1 The Great North Run is a regular and recurring half marathon held each September between Newcastle-upon-Tyne and South Shields in north-east England

> **Exam tip**
>
> To gain the most marks in your exam, make sure that you can correctly distinguish between the three types of major sporting events stated on the syllabus (i.e. regular, one-off, regular and recurring).

3.1.2 The nature of the participants and spectators

Lots of major sporting events have an international element, with sports performers and spectators travelling to compete in or watch them from two or more countries. This helps to ensure a global spectator audience and worldwide media coverage. International events that meet the criteria of involving participants and spectators from two or more countries include the:

+ Olympic Games
+ Paralympic Games
+ Netball World Cup
+ Formula 1 Grand Prix races
+ Commonwealth Games
+ African Cup of Nations
+ Asian Games.

> **Now test yourself** TESTED
>
> + Write down as many major sporting events as you can think of in 60 seconds.
> + Take this list, divide a sheet of paper into three columns and identify whether each of the events you have written down occurs i) regularly; ii) as a one-off; or iii) on a regular and recurring basis.

International A major sporting event involving participants and spectators from two or more countries.

> **Typical mistake**
>
> Avoid mixing up the meaning and correct use of examples of the different types and scheduling of major sporting events (e.g. writing 'regular events are annual and take place in the same place every year, for example the FA Cup Final' would be incorrect).

Check your understanding and progress at www.hoddereducation.co.uk/myrevisionnotes

> **Check your understanding**
>
> 1 Define what is meant by a 'regular event', a 'one-off event' and a 'regular and recurring event', then give an example for each.
> 2 Read the following statements and decide whether you think they are true or false:
>   a A regular sports event is one which is held every four years.
>   b A one-off sports event is held in a host city once in a generation.
>   c The Wimbledon Tennis Championships are an example of a regular and recurring sports event.
>   d The FA Cup is an example of a regular and recurring sports event.
>   e A regular and recurring sports event is one that is held annually at the same venue.
> 3 Give three examples of international sporting events which involve performers and spectators from two or more countries.
> 4 Match up the following sporting events and their descriptions.
>
> | Sporting event | | Description | |
> |---|---|---|---|
> | i | Olympic Games | a | Annual Championship game of the National Football League |
> | ii | Super Bowl | b | More than 200 nations competing in over 30 different sports in different venues every four years |
> | iii | ICC Cricket World Cup | c | Organised by UEFA, the most prestigious club tournament in European club football |
> | iv | Champions League Final | d | Held annually at the All England Club in London |
> | v | Wimbledon Tennis Championships | e | The premier international event for men's one-day international cricket |

3.2 Positive and negative pre-event aspects of hosting a major sporting event

REVISED

3.2.1 Positive and negative pre-event aspects of hosting a major sporting event

There are various aspects of hosting a major sporting event, which may be viewed either positively or negatively. These include bidding for the event, which might raise local or national objections, and the infrastructure and transport system development required when hosting. In addition, the financial and commercial investment required to host a major sporting event can be viewed both positively and negatively, as can the possible job creation and increased employment opportunities associated with acting as a host.

It is very costly to bid to host a major sporting event, and for the bidder to demonstrate that they have the ability to host it successfully. This is certainly the case with the Olympic and Paralympic Games, as well as major global sporting events such as the FIFA World Cup which cost the Russian Government $11.8 billion in construction and preparation costs alone. The high cost of bidding and hosting means that only a few countries can be considered to host major sporting events.

Potential host countries or cities have to think very carefully before deciding whether or not to enter the bidding process for a major sporting event because, while there are a number of possible reasons for doing so, there are also potential reasons not to. These are explored in detail in Table 3.1.

> **Infrastructure** The basic physical and organisational structures and facilities (e.g. buildings, roads and power supplies) needed for the operation of a society or enterprise.

Table 3.1 Positive and negative pre-event aspects of hosting a major sporting event

Possible reasons for bidding to host a major sporting event	Possible reasons against bidding to host a major sporting event
Social benefits Bidding countries/cities receive increased status or recognition as a result of entering the bidding process	**High financial costs** There are many costs associated with bidding, even if the bid is ultimately unsuccessful (e.g. Chicago spent $100 million on its 2016 Olympic bid but lost out to Rio) There are financial risks involved in bidding, even when successful (e.g. Atlanta spent $600 million to complement existing infrastructure in their winning bid to host the 1996 Olympic Games)
Economic benefits Worldwide attention allows countries/cities to stimulate their economy, with the expectation of commercial investment and increased trade and tourism Positive publicity associated with a bid (e.g. via media coverage publicising the economic benefits of hosting) can increase public support for the high investment required Bidding can generate increased anticipation for job creation with lots of potential employment opportunities (e.g. when bidding for the 2016 Olympic and Paralympic Games, Chicago and Rio both had the aim of increasing tourism and developing infrastructure and investment, which would last well beyond the staging of the Games. Chicago wanted to use media exposure from the bid to address transportation, security and international tourism needs)	**Low-level economic development** Bids in poorer, less-developed countries may meet with local or national opposition if people think the money could be better spent on greater social needs (e.g. health care, social housing or education)
Development of infrastructure and transport systems Potential to create a positive vision and plan, and a long-lasting **legacy** of improved transport systems (e.g. air, rail and road) Improvements in infrastructure before the event begins can increase public excitement and support	**Lack of public support** High costs associated with bidding and/or hosting, such as for the development of infrastructure and transport systems, may not generate public support (e.g. Boston, USA, pulled out of the bidding process for the 2024 Olympics due to 'people power' and protests by their citizens group 'No Boston Olympics') There may be local and/or national objections due to the potential environmental impact of putting in place the necessary infrastructure/sports venues for such an event
Positive legacy Desire for legacy (e.g. regeneration of run-down areas; plans for new housing, shops, hospitals, etc.; building new sports facilities for use during and after an event) can increase public support	**Negative legacy (e.g. non-use of facilities)** If not effectively planned for at the bidding stage, new sports facilities may be at risk of minimal/low-level use after the event (e.g. Nigeria built a $300 million 60,000-seat stadium for the 2003 African Games, but the high maintenance required, the surrounding infrastructure and a high crime rate in the area mean that the stadium remains empty; South Korea built ten new stadiums holding between 40,000 and 60,000 fans for the 2002 World Cup – their average crowd size is around 3,000, leaving lots of empty terraces in the grounds and only five of the ten stadiums built are still in use)
Sporting benefits Building new sports facilities could lead to increased participation in sport at a grassroots level New facilities will support elite performers requiring specialist centres for training and competing	

Check your understanding and progress at www.hoddereducation.co.uk/myrevisionnotes

Figure 3.2 The London 2012 Olympic Stadium is now home to West Ham United

As a result of the potential negative aspects of bidding for a major sporting event, the numbers of countries/cities bidding have been in decline (e.g. 2004 Olympics – twelve cities bid; 2020 Olympics – five cities bid). The International Olympic Committee (IOC) reacted to this decrease by making the bidding process more affordable in an attempt to encourage more countries to participate in it.

Legacy That which is left behind.

> **Now test yourself** TESTED
>
> Watch the following clip: 'Why Hosting The Olympics Isn't Worth It Anymore'
>
> https://www.youtube.com/watch?v=0bXJGZgR1BU
>
> Note down the positive and negative aspects of bidding for and hosting an Olympic Games.

> **Check your understanding**
>
> 5 How can bidding for a major sporting event benefit a country in sporting terms?
> 6 Why might local or national objections be made to the bidding process for a major sporting event?

Benefits Positive outcomes which result from hosting a major sporting event.

Drawbacks Negative outcomes which result from hosting a major sporting event.

3.3 Potential positive and negative aspects of hosting a major sporting event

REVISED

3.3.1 During the event

Hosting major sporting events such as the FIFA World Cup or the Olympic/Paralympic Games can have a number of potential positives or benefits as well as possible negatives or drawbacks.

Positive aspects/benefits of hosting
+ Improved social infrastructure.
+ Improved national morale/social cohesion.
+ An increase in national status.
+ Greater national interest in sport.
+ Increased media coverage of the sport(s).
+ A potential increase in direct tourism and indirect tourism.
+ An increase in short-term employment during the event.

Social infrastructure The fundamental services and structures that support the quality of life of a nation or neighbourhood (e.g. transport services such as pedestrian areas or cycle lanes; venues and public spaces for recreation, such as playgrounds, skateboard parks and outdoor basketball courts).

Social cohesion The set of characteristics that mean a group is able to function as a unit.

> **Exam tip**
>
> If a question asks for the positive and/or negative impacts of hosting a major sporting event during that event, to earn marks your answer must relate to impacts experienced while actually staging the event. Discussing longer-term (i.e. legacy) aspects of hosting a major sporting event won't gain you any marks.

My Revision Notes Cambridge National Level 1/Level 2 in Sport Studies Second Edition

Improved social infrastructure

+ Improved infrastructure/social infrastructure (e.g. pedestrianised areas, cycle lanes, road/tram systems or railway networks, community and social housing, shopping centres and hotels) may be built as a result of hosting a major sporting event. This will benefit people who live in or visit the area where the events are staged.
+ There may be increased investment in the development and/or improvement of the transport system to help cope with the increased numbers of visitors and spectators expected to visit before, during and after the event.
+ There may be increased investment in the local area (i.e. regeneration).
+ Investment in local transport and/or road networks may result in the economic regeneration of an area (e.g. the Javelin railway to the London Olympic Stadium is an example of a better road network).
+ More public spaces may be created to increase the opportunities to mix socially while participating in physical activity or recreation activities (e.g. parks, playgrounds, skate parks). The site of the Olympic Park from London 2012 has been transformed into a large public space – Queen Elizabeth Parkland – and used by millions over the years.

Improved national morale/social cohesion

+ When the population of a country gets behind and celebrates the successes of their elite athletes, it can result in improved national morale and/or a feeling of social cohesion (i.e. increased integration/unity within a country). This might be shown via flag waving.

Increase in national status

+ Successfully hosting a major sporting event will raise the status of a city or country as people get to see and hear about it via global media coverage (e.g. Brazil/Rio in 2016); the shop window effect is a positive outcome for successful hosts of major global sporting events.

Greater national interest in sport

+ **Sports facilities may be improved or developed/built:** World-class sporting venues are often developed for major sporting events, resulting in better facilities for the nation after the event. As these facilities can be used by both elite athletes and recreational performers, there is often an increased interest in sport (e.g. Beijing's Bird's Nest Stadium was developed into a winter wonderland; London's Olympic stadium was converted into a multi-purpose venue/football stadium; Eton Manor was converted into a hockey and tennis centre).
+ **Increased participation in sports as a result of watching sports performers:** Hosting major sporting events increases spectatorship and participation rates (e.g. there was increased popularity in rugby union after the Rugby World Cup in 2015; there were increased participation rates in cycling after the London 2012 Olympics; spectator numbers for women's tennis increased following Emma Raducanu's success in the US Open in 2021).
+ **Increased participation in sports as a result of awareness of role models:** Major sporting events can lead to an increase of and greater diversity in elite role models (e.g. Mo Farrah winning gold at the London 2012 Olympics).
+ **Increased funding allocated to sports:** Sports attract more funding in the lead up to a major sporting event from government grants, the National Lottery, sponsorship deals and organisations like Sport England and UK Sport (e.g. there was increased funding for women's rugby union via UK Sport Lottery funding in the lead-up to the Olympics). This funding can be used to develop grassroots participation (e.g. British Cycling organising the Sky Ride programme).

> **Typical mistake**
>
> Do not forget to learn both positive and negative pre-event aspects of hosting a major sporting event. It is easy to lose marks by focusing on negative pre-event aspects of hosting a major sporting event when the question clearly requires answers that 'discuss' both positive and negative aspects.

> **Regeneration** The improvement of and appropriate investment in facilities or delivery of services in poor neighbourhoods and the empowerment of local communities in processes aimed at bringing an area 'back to life'.
>
> **Shop window effect** The increased status of a country resulting from successful hosting of major global sporting events.

Check your understanding and progress at www.hoddereducation.co.uk/myrevisionnotes

Figure 3.3 Emma Raducanu's success at the US Open in 2021 increased spectator numbers for women's tennis

Increased media coverage of the sport(s)
+ TV stations like the BBC and Sky TV bid to cover different sports during major sporting events.
+ Participation rates may increase in some sports due to increased media coverage during major sporting events (e.g. there was an increase in BMX participation due to the London 2012 Olympics).
+ Increased media coverage may lead to greater numbers of spectators because of the additional viewing platforms (e.g. more people chose to watch netball on Sky after England's success in the 2018 Commonwealth Games in Australia, which was shown on TV).

A potential increase in direct and indirect tourism
+ Direct tourism involves people visiting the host city or country as a result of attending the major sporting event, while indirect tourism results from visitors visiting the host city or country after the event because they have been made aware of it via global media coverage.
+ Increased tourism during an event generates revenue in economic sectors such as retail, hospitality and accommodation (e.g. money spent in local hotels, bars or restaurants), as well as increased revenue from merchandise sales, etc. and from tourist visits to other local attractions (e.g. more people may visit Mount Fuji or Hiroshima while in Japan for the Rugby World Cup).

> **Direct tourism** People who visit a host city or country as a result of attending the major sporting event.
>
> **Indirect tourism** People who visit a host city or country after the event having been made aware of it via global media coverage.

An increase in short-term employment during the event
+ A range of jobs and/or employment opportunities may be created, resulting in a stronger economy (e.g. increases in construction, retail or hospitality industries may mean a need for more staff for hotels and restaurants or in security jobs). Note that many of these positions may only be short term.

Other financial benefits
+ **Increased commercial benefits for local businesses:** Businesses may benefit due to an increased customer base or the creation of new businesses (e.g. travel companies increasing sales).
+ **Admission charges/ticket sales:** Revenue is generated by the sale of tickets to view matches or events during a major sporting event (e.g. there are 64 matches during the Football World Cup, which generates lots of revenue through ticket sales).

+ **New facilities may generate income:** Admission charges resulting from public use after the event will generate additional revenue (e.g. the velodrome being opened to the general public after the Olympic Games).

Negative aspects/drawbacks of hosting
+ An increase in transport, litter and noise as a result of increased transport or tourism.
+ The potential for an increase in terrorism and crime.
+ Poor performance by the home nation/team and the impact on national pride/morale (e.g. if there is an early exit from a competition by home-based performers).
+ Perceived relegation/lack of investment in regional areas not involved in the national event – this may cause divisions within a country if the specific area hosting it (i.e. a city such as London in the 2012 Olympics) is seen as the only beneficiary and other areas of the country lose out or fail to see the benefits of being a host. People may also resent the use of public taxes to fund an event in one area of the country as opposed to investing in other areas of society that are more in need (e.g. health or education).
+ Negative media coverage of perceived deficiencies in the organisation or infrastructure/facilities (e.g. facilities not being built on time, low ticket sales and lots of empty seats during the event).
+ High costs of hosting the event can be more than the revenue raised, leaving the hosts in debt or financial difficulty (e.g. the debts of the 1976 **Montreal Olympics** are reported to have taken 30 years for taxpayers to pay off).
+ Hosting an event focused on a single sport (e.g. the Cricket World Cup) may only help to promote that sport and others may suffer as a consequence.
+ Disorganised or poorly run events can have a negative impact on the status of a country; this is also true if public perception of an event is negatively affected by the threat of terrorism or controversy (e.g. political demonstrations in Brazil/Rio in 2016).
+ Economic benefits or jobs created as a result of hosting may only be temporary/short term.

> **Montreal Olympics** The 1976 Summer Olympics, officially called the Games of the XXI Olympiad, was an international multi-sport event in Montreal, Canada, in 1976, and the first Olympic Games held in Canada.

> **Check your understanding**
>
> 7 Explain the difference between direct and indirect tourism as a result of hosting a major sports event.
>
> 8 Outline how poor performance by home athletes could affect a host nation.

> **Exam tip**
>
> If the command word 'discuss' is used in a question about the impact on a host city or country of staging a major international sporting event, make sure you provide positive points as well as negative points (i.e. give a balanced answer).

3.3.2 Immediate and longer term post-event

Positive aspects/benefits
Examples of positive aspects/benefits of being a host immediately and longer term post-event include:
+ a legacy of improved/new sporting facilities
+ an increase in participation in sports
+ an increase in the profile of sports involved
+ a legacy of improved transport and social infrastructure
+ raising of the city's or nation's international profile or status
+ an increase in future financial investment
+ tourism may increase after the event (e.g. returning to the country for a holiday at a later date).

Negative aspects/drawbacks
Examples of negative aspects/drawbacks of being a host immediately and longer term post-event include:
+ the event might have cost more to host than the revenue generated
+ sports facilities are unused after the event

> **Typical mistake**
>
> Avoid writing answers with too much repetition of words or phrases that already appear in the question. For example, writing 'there will be *economic and sporting benefits* as a result of hosting a major sporting event' will not earn any marks if these benefits are part of the question set.

- a loss in national reputation or status if the event was badly organised, the host nation's participants performed badly or scandals emerged
- the participation legacy (i.e. increased participation in the general population) may be limited; increased participation does not always result from hosting major sporting events
- sporting facilities may be underused or not used at all after the event if the planning of an event is not carefully thought through; this means there is the possibility of a negative legacy (e.g. Barcelona's 1992 diving pool).

Check your understanding

9 Identify reasons why hosting a major sporting event might lower a country's national reputation.

10 Identify the potential long-term drawbacks of hosting a major sporting event.

Exam checklist

In this section you learned about the features of a major sporting event and the implications for a city or country of hosting a major sporting event. These features and implications include:
- the types and scheduling of major sporting events (regular, one-off, and regular and recurring)
- examples of major sporting events applied to the different types and scheduling of major sporting events
- the international nature of the participants and spectators in major sporting events
- the positive and negative pre-event aspects of hosting a major sporting event, including the bidding process
- the potential positive and negative aspects of hosting a major sporting event during the event itself
- the potential longer-term positive and negative legacy effects of hosting a major sporting event.

Exam-style questions

1 Define what is meant by the following terms:
   a One-off events
   b Regular events
   c Regular and recurring events [3]

2 Give three examples of regular major sporting events that are normally hosted in different cities every year.
   a _____
   b _____
   c _____ [3]

3 Identify three different examples of 'one-off events'.
   a _____
   b _____
   c _____ [3]

4 Identify whether hosting the following sporting events are one-off, regular or regular and recurring by completing the table below. [6]

Sporting event	One-off	Regular	Regular and recurring
Asian Games			
UEFA Champions League Final			
FA Cup Final			
Paralympics			
Formula 1 British Grand Prix			
London Marathon			

5 Outline the positive and negative pre-event aspects of hosting a major sporting event. [6]

6 Outline the potential negative aspects of hosting a major sporting event, such as the Rugby World Cup. [4]

7 Hosting a major sports event such as the Olympics can have a number of positive and negative effects on a host city and country. Describe an example for each of the following:
   a Positive financial effect:
   b Negative financial effect:
   c Positive effect on facilities:
   d Negative effect on facilities: [4]

8 Complete the following table identifying possible negative aspects of hosting major sporting events linked to the positive ones already stated. [5]

Positive aspects	Negative aspects
Increased tourism	
Increased job opportunities	
Development of new sports facilities	
Increased participation in sport	
Improved morale	

9 Identify the benefits to a country of hosting a major sporting event *during* the event. [4]

10 Using examples, explain the possible benefits for a country hosting a major sporting event such as the multi-sport Olympic Games or the single-sport rugby union World Cup. [8]

My Revision Notes Cambridge National Level 1/Level 2 in Sport Studies Second Edition

Topic area 4: The role National Governing Bodies (NGBs) play in the development of their sport

4.1 National Governing Bodies (NGBs)

REVISED

4.1.1 What NGBs do for their sport

National Governing Bodies (NGBs) are independent bodies that operate in a country. They have a 'sport-specific focus' and ensure that lots of different functions are fulfilled in relation to that sport.

Examples of different NGBs and their *focus sports* (i.e. the sport(s) they are responsible for) include the following:
+ Football Association (FA)
+ Rugby Football Union (RFU)
+ England Netball
+ England Hockey
+ England Basketball
+ Lawn Tennis Association (LTA)
+ British Swimming – swimming/open water swimming, water polo, synchro swimming and diving.

NGBs fulfil a variety of different functions in relation to sport as reflected in their key areas of involvement. These are outlined and explained below.

> **National Governing Bodies (NGBs)**
> Independent, self-appointed organisations that govern their sports through the common consent of their sport.

> **Check your understanding**
> 1 What are National Governing Bodies?
> 2 Identify the six NGBs for the following sports:
>   Surfing: _____
>   Boxing: _____
>   Handball: _____
>   Badminton: _____
>   Cycling: _____
>   Rounders: _____
> 3 List six different NGBs and the sports they are responsible for, in addition to those identified in question 2 above.

Promote participation

A major role of NGBs is to promote their sport and increase its popularity. NGBs can promote participation through various schemes and initiatives, and by ensuring as much media coverage as possible for their focus sport.

They can also increase participation by developing and applying policies and practices on *equal opportunities* and by promoting participation in the sport it is responsible for to all sections of the community (i.e. all genders, religions, cultures, ages and ability levels).

If an NGB wishes to promote its sport to women, for example, it could use a number of different strategies such as:
- using/involving themselves in promotional campaigns (e.g. 'This Girl Can')
- providing equal access to sports facilities (e.g. via equal opportunities policies)
- providing taster sessions/women-only sessions in sports such as boxing
- ensuring media coverage promotes female role models
- training and developing more female sports coaches and officials in their sport.

Examples of NGBs who are working hard to try and achieve equality/inclusivity in their sport and increase its popularity include:
- the FA – who are working co-operatively with a range of other organisations including 'Kick It Out' to challenge racism in football at all levels of participation from grassroots to professionals
- England Netball – who are developing and applying a ParaNetball strategy for disability participation in netball that aims to understand, engage, maximise and empower deaf and disabled women and girls across England.

NGBs can also increase the popularity of a sport via participation schemes, some of which are promoted in schools. For example:
- Netball's 'High 5' programme is a specially designed version of the sport for 9–11-year-old children and has an emphasis on fun
- Football's Premier League 'Primary Stars' programme aims to inspire children aged 5–11 to learn to be more physically active via links to Premier League football clubs
- British Cycling's HSBC UK 'Ready Set Ride' is working with the Youth Sport Trust to bring cycling to new generations by empowering families and school communities to help children learn to ride a bike
- Badminton England's 'The Racket Pack' (for 5–11 year olds) and 'SmashUp!' (for 11–16 year olds) programmes, which are aimed at primary and secondary school children and have an emphasis on fun
- Table Tennis England's 'Loop at Work', 'Ping!' and 'TT Kidz' initiatives aim to make table tennis more accessible and to inspire a new generation of players.

Figure 4.1 All Stars Cricket is an initiative between an NGB (England and Wales Cricket Board) that supports children learning cricket

> **Now test yourself**
>
> Research how an NGB of your choice is trying to achieve equality and inclusivity. A good way of doing this is to visit the website of your chosen NGB (e.g. Table Tennis England's website is https://tabletennisengland.co.uk/).
>
> Produce a bullet-point summary of the strategies being used by the NGB you have chosen.
>
> TESTED

Youth Sport Trust A national charity dedicated to building a brighter future for all young people.

> **Typical mistake**
>
> Students often lose marks by not providing examples of NGB participation schemes when a question specifically requires it (e.g. 'Using examples…').

> **Check your understanding**
>
> 4 Identify two initiatives being used by Badminton England to increase participation by school-aged children.
> 5 Identify the strategies an NGB could use to increase gender equality in sport.

NGBs can also promote their sport via increased media exposure and/or publicity, or by raising the profile of their sport in the following ways:

+ increasing awareness of potential participants (e.g. on the TV/radio or in newspapers) – examples could include regular press releases via media/social media officers about recent or upcoming events (e.g. community engagement projects where elite performers visit schools/sports clubs)
+ increasing awareness of where to play sport by promoting sports clubs and their facilities, and advertising sporting initiatives in a particular sport in a targeted area.

Rugby union and cricket both benefited from increased media exposure after successes in the twenty-first century, which has generated a higher profile for the sports and increased participation.

> **Community engagement**
> A way of developing a working relationship between public bodies (such as local councils/schools) and community groups.

Develop the sport's coaching and officiating infrastructure

NGBs are responsible for the development of sports-specific coaching awards and/or qualifications with different levels of structure to follow. For example:

+ England Netball have a coaching pathway as follows: England Netball Level 1 → England Netball Level 2 → England Netball Level 3 (the highest level of coaching qualification available in netball across England)
+ England Badminton's coaching pathway includes: Foundation Award in Coaching Badminton → Coach Award in Coaching Badminton → UKCC Level 3 Certificate for Head Coach in Badminton.

NGBs play a key role in training and selecting officials to officiate at different levels of the sport they are responsible for, as in the following examples:

+ The RFU use a 'Young Officials Award' as a starting point to encourage more young people into officiating and provide a structure to progress through (e.g. beyond introductory awards there are other levels to work through to improve understanding of the detailed laws of the sport and how to enforce them correctly in competition).
+ The first step on England Netball's officiating pathway is the 'Into Officiating Course'. It is designed to aid understanding of the basic rules of the game, as well as covering some of the basic positioning and movement required to enable officials to 'whistle well' while being an umpire. The course is designed for people new to umpiring and new to the rules of the game. Next stages include: C Award Umpire Course → B Award Umpire Course → A Award Umpire Course. There is also a 'Technical Officials Course' for those wanting to train in scoring and timing netball matches.

> **Exam tip**
> To gain the most marks in your exam, make sure you can identify and illustrate NGB coaching and officiating qualifications that are available in a particular sport.

> **Now test yourself** TESTED
>
> Research how an NGB of your choice provides coaching and officiating opportunities and progression. A good way of doing this is to visit the website of your chosen NGB (e.g. Badminton England's website is www.badmintonengland.co.uk and England Netball's website is www.englandnetball.co.uk).
>
> Produce a bullet-point summary of the examples you have found.

> **Check your understanding**
>
> 6 Outline the pathway/structure England Netball are using to develop officials in their sport.
> 7 Outline the coaching pathway Badminton England have developed for their sport.

Organise tournaments and competitions

NGBs help to support and organise competitions from grassroots local club level (e.g. local leagues) through to elite level, such as National Schools, National Clubs and Para Sport events (e.g. see the England Netball website). Table Tennis England, for example, are responsible for organising competitions and the tournament structure for table tennis in England from grassroots through to the elite level national championships as outlined below:

+ National Cadet and Junior League (aimed at grassroots players)
+ Team and individual competitions for schools
+ English Leagues Cup Competitions
+ County Championships
+ Inter-Regionals
+ Grand Prix events
+ British League
+ National Championships
+ 1*–4* competitions.

> **Check your understanding**
>
> 8 Identify four competitions Table Tennis England organise for participants in their sport.

> **Exam tip**
>
> To gain the most marks in your exam, make sure you can give current examples of tournaments or competitions organised by NGBs.

Amend the existing rules and apply disciplinary procedures for rule breaking

NGBs are responsible for the development of rules for their sport and for applying disciplinary procedures for rule breaking. For example:

+ rule-making and the organisation of drugs testing
+ the development of and enforcement of disciplinary procedures (e.g. the FA have procedures in place which apply to any individual or team playing football, and England Hockey provide detailed advice via their website of their disciplinary procedures and ways in which players can appeal against any decisions made against them)
+ the development of rules in conjunction with those which apply internationally (e.g. the RFU develop rules in line with those of the World Rugby Executive Committee).

Some sports have recently changed some of their rules and regulations, for example:

+ golf – new rules include changes to the dropping procedure, measuring in taking relief, removing the penalty for a double hit and balls lost or out of bounds
+ football – there are new rules for penalties, drop balls, goal-kicks, substitutions and cards for coaches.

> **Now test yourself** TESTED
>
> Watch the R&A's video '20 Must Know Rules of Golf Changes for 2019' at: https://www.youtube.com/watch?v=toqwshRGe4g
>
> Note down the various rule changes made to try and make golf a more exciting and appealing sport to play.

As mentioned, NGBs also need to apply disciplinary procedures for rule breaking. The FA typically deal with the following:
+ lots of aggressive/insulting behaviour and abusive language aimed at match officials from players, managers and coaches
+ mass confrontations and failures by clubs to control players
+ misconduct in relation to betting
+ misconduct in relation to social media posts.

The sanctions imposed for such offences include fines of various amounts, touchline bans and suspensions of varying lengths.

The disciplinary procedure in rugby union is as follows. On receipt of a written complaint from a member, another team within the sport, the governing body, the league/match organisers or any other party, the Elected Officers, with advice from a Legal Advisor should they so wish, will decide whether the complaint falls within the scope of this disciplinary code.

Further procedures and measures to be taken are outlined in 'RFU Regulation 19' which provides the framework for dealing with all disciplinary matters.

> **Sanction** A threatened penalty for disobeying a rule or law in sport.
>
> **Safeguarding** Actions taken for the welfare of children to ensure they are protected from harm.

Now test yourself

TESTED

Visit the FA website link below and research then note down the different football disciplinary cases they reviewed in a 'typical month' (i.e. May–June 2021) and the sanctions given.

www.thefa.com/football-rules-governance/discipline/suspensions

Check your understanding

9 Who could potentially be disciplined by an NGB for rule infringements?

> **Exam tip**
>
> To help ensure you earn the most marks in your exam, make sure you are aware of recent and current rule changes, and the disciplinary measures implemented by NGBs for rule infringement.

Ensure safety within their sport

NGBs are responsible for ensuring safety within their sport. Safeguarding is an area NGBs have had to become increasingly aware of due to a number of high-profile cases of child abuse in sport which have hit the media headlines (e.g. by football coaches at professional clubs such as Southampton, Peterborough United and Crewe Alexandra). NGBs have a very important role to play in providing appropriate access to advice and procedures in order to ensure the safeguarding of children (e.g. via training modules as part of coaching awards).

A number of NGBs have been required to undertake independent/internal inquiries following allegations of unsafe or unequal practice in their sport. For example:
+ British Cycling – Jess Varnish and other cyclists raised concerns alleging sexism and disability discrimination
+ British Gymnastics – a large number of safeguarding issues were raised in July 2020, which led to an independent enquiry into a number of bullying/abuse allegations (including 'fat shaming') made by a number of gymnasts against British Gymnastics staff.

Examples of NGB guiding principles for safeguarding include the following:
+ England Handball recommend that any coach leading or coaching youth age groups in a solo capacity should have a valid DBS Check, a minimum Level 1 coaching qualification and have completed a UK coaching Safeguarding and Protecting Children workshop.
+ Rounders England have a clear policy on safeguarding children which states that they aim to protect and promote the welfare of all young people in rounders to ensure that they can enjoy the sport free from all forms of abuse and exploitation.

> **DBS** The Disclosure and Barring Service is a non-departmental public body of the Home Office of the United Kingdom. A DBS check is carried out to make sure a potential coach has no criminal record relating to safeguarding issues.

Check your understanding and progress at www.hoddereducation.co.uk/myrevisionnotes

> **Now test yourself** TESTED ⭕
>
> Visit an NGB website and research how it promotes and ensures safeguarding in the sport it is responsible for. Some examples are given below but there are many more you could choose.
> + Rounders England: https://www.roundersengland.co.uk/safeguarding/
> + Table Tennis England: https://tabletennisengland.co.uk/our-sport/safeguarding/
> + British Cycling: https://www.britishcycling.org.uk/safeguarding/

Provide support, insurance and technical guidance to members

NGBs are responsible for providing support, insurance and technical guidance to their members. They also provide different types of policies and initiatives for more general support (e.g. via their websites and/or NGB helplines). Examples of such support include the following:

+ Insurance: a number of NGBs have an area of their website that only official members can access. This area provides legal advice, guidelines and information about how members can access support and get themselves insured (e.g. via links to insurance companies with whom the NGB has developed connections or endorsed products). Registered members of British Gymnastics can access insurance which is specifically designed to protect individuals when taking part in the sport (e.g. in June 2021 it was W Denis Insurance Brokers).
+ Health and safety: another service provided by British Gymnastics is their association with Agility UK which provides all club members with a dedicated health and safety advice service.
+ Assistance with facility development: NGBs are an important source of expert advice on facility design and development, whether at international level or at grassroots sports clubs. NGBs are often seen as experts in providing valuable advice/assistance to grassroots sports clubs when they are applying for funding to develop their facilities (e.g. Sport England and their 'Inspired Facilities' scheme).
+ Technical advice: this refers to NGB advice given about equipment (e.g. safety equipment), venues and surfaces (e.g. information about artificial surfaces).
+ Location and contact details for local clubs and advice on how to get started/involved in the sport: this often takes the form of a directory organised into regions/counties with information including directions to a club, the age ranges catered for at a club, and when starter/taster events are being held (e.g. England Basketball's 'find a court' website).

NGBs also support the development of their sport at elite level and locally (within a community). This is explored in Table 4.1.

> **Inspired Facilities** A scheme which focused on making it easier for local community and volunteer groups to improve and refurbish sports clubs or transform non-sporting venues into modern grassroots sport facilities.
>
> **Talent ID** The process of recognising current players or performers that have the potential to excel within a sport.

Table 4.1 NGB support for development of sport at elite and local levels

Development of sport at elite level	Development of sport at local/community level
Providing national performance centres	Organising competitions and tournaments
Organising national performance squads, elite training camps or access to elite coaching	Providing funding to clubs
Training high-level coaches and officials	Providing resources and guidance on coaching/coaching awards
Providing funding support to elite level performers (e.g. squads and teams)	Providing advice on facilities and sources of funding for facility development
Developing Talent ID schemes	Providing advice on safeguarding
Providing a clear progression pathway to elite level sport	Training and providing officials
	Providing insurance to members
	Providing a central handbook and/or contact details for local clubs an individual may wish to join

> **Exam tip**
>
> Questions on NGBs typically score low marks so it is worth learning and revising this section in as much detail as possible so you can gain an advantage over other students sitting the exam at the same time as you.

> **Check your understanding**
>
> 10 Give two examples of support, insurance or technical guidance that NGBs provide for their members.

Develop policies and initiatives

NGBs are responsible for the development of policies and initiatives to improve their sport in the best ways possible and set the direction and vision of that sport in their country. Policies developed by NGBs include the following:

+ **Anti-doping policies and guidance:** the England and Wales Cricket Board's (ECB) anti-doping policy clearly identifies a list of substances which are permitted and those which are banned. The British Gymnastics website includes a section which provides detailed information on which drugs are banned, procedures for testing, and advice on nutritional supplements and what is acceptable as a therapeutic use exemption (TUE).
+ **Promoting excellence and fair play:** an important role of an NGB is to promote high levels of etiquette and fair play. The FA set up its 'Respect' campaign to improve the behaviour of coaches and parents, etc. and encourage them to act as positive role models to others involved in playing the game. It has been developed into 'We only do positive' to try and ensure that football is played in a fun, safe and inclusive environment.
+ **Community programmes:** NGBs involve themselves in community engagement schemes/initiatives. Such schemes aim to encourage participation via fun/active learning and involvement in a sport (e.g. the Amateur Swimming Association (ASA) have developed the 'Swimfit' programme, which gives members of the community a chance to access an online coach to help them use swimming to get fit and to complete a variety of different challenges). The FA have lots of community/grassroots projects, such as those sponsored by McDonald's which include 'Fun Football Festivals' and 'The FA Super-Kicks'.
+ **Development:** Another very important role of an NGB is to ensure performers are able to develop via clear, progressive pathways. British Gymnastic's 'Performance Pathway Programme for Trampoline' is an example of a structured route participants can progress through. It involves a series of challenging, educational and engaging training camps to identify some of the best current performers and to teach them about the physical and mental skills they will need for success.

NGBs can develop performers in a sport in a number of different ways. Examples include the following:

+ **Elite performer training and development:** NGBs can provide national performance squads, the selection of national teams, the organisation of elite training camps, etc.
+ **Central contracts:** in 2018 the ECB awarded annual central contracts to ten male test players and thirteen white ball – ODI/T20 male players; 21 central contracts were awarded by the ECB for England Women for 2019.

Anti-doping Preventing the use of illegal PEDs.

Therapeutic use exemption (TUE) The process by which an athlete can obtain official approval to use a prescribed prohibited substance or method for the treatment of a legitimate medical condition.

Pathways Structured routes for performers to progress through.

Central contracts Elite Player Squad (EPS) agreements.

- **Coaching awards:** the development of an NGB coaching structure (e.g. following the UK Coaching Certificate (UKCC) structure from Level 1 to Level 3).
- **Training of officials:** all NGBs offer officiating pathways starting from Level 1, which can be accessed by individuals wanting to get involved in this aspect of sport
- **Providing a national directive and vision:** all NGBs must provide direction and vision for their sport in a country. The LTA vision is to provide support to as many people as possible to help them enjoy tennis and get involved with playing it.

> **Check your understanding**
>
> 11 Define what is meant by a therapeutic use exemption (TUE).

> **Exam tip**
>
> To gain the most marks in your exam, make sure you can illustrate your awareness of how an NGB develops its policies and initiatives.

Lobby for funding

NGBs are responsible for providing advice and support to members looking to access funding in order to improve provision. NGB websites often include advice to members in that particular sport on how to apply for funding (e.g. performers/club officials).

NGBs and sports clubs require money/income in order to operate. There are a number of ways they can lobby for and get funding, as illustrated by the following list of potential sources:
- UK Sport for elite performer investment
- Sport England
- grants/government funding
- membership/national affiliation fees
- subscription/match fees
- National Lottery/UK Sport funding
- media/TV rights
- income from sponsorship/advertising (e.g. via corporate partners such as the FA and Vauxhall; Rugby League and First Utility)
- donations
- merchandising
- admission charges/ticket sales
- NGB initiatives (e.g. Football Foundation).

Having generated lots of income/money, NGBs then have to decide how to spend it (i.e. distribute it). NGBs distribute their funds to a variety of different sources, including the following:
- grants/funding awards to individual performers
- funding to help elite performers compete successfully in international sports events
- funding of grassroots schemes/initiatives (e.g. in sports clubs)
- education/schools
- community engagement
- funding of sports venue/facility development
- funding of user groups to increase participation in under-represented groups of the community (e.g. minority ethnic groups).

There are lots of different ways in which a sports club could spend NGB funding they receive to help them overcome a number of different barriers, as illustrated in Table 4.2.

> **Football Foundation** The United Kingdom's largest sports charity, which channels funding from the Premier League, the FA and the Government to transform the landscape of grassroots sport in England.

Table 4.2 Spending NGB funding to overcome barriers

Barrier	Strategy/initiative
Cost	Subsidise/offer discounted sessions
Lack of awareness	Publicise via investment in print media (e.g. leaflets/posters) and social media
Lack of access to facilities/specialist equipment/lack of transport	Invest in private free/adapted transport and specialist equipment
Lack of specialist/good quality facilities	Finance the provision of specialist/better quality facilities
Lack of role models	Pay for use of positive role models to promote a sport (e.g. at a promotional or taster event)
Media stereotypes	Provide evidence of role models to challenge stereotypes
Lack of time	Invest in crèche/childcare provision; provide a flexible programme of activities
Work restrictions	Finance work-based clubs/longer opening hours at sports clubs, etc.
Discrimination	Invest in anti-discrimination organisations and initiatives

Now test yourself

TESTED

Research online how an NGB of your choice is achieving its 'role', including how they are promoting participation, and funding and developing the sport and its coaching and officiating infrastructure. Look for examples of policies and initiatives the NGB is currently promoting.

Exam tip

To gain the most marks in your exam, make sure you can give examples of how an NGB generates its funding.

Check your understanding

12 Identify six different ways an NGB can help a sports club generate funding.

13 NGBs have various roles when supporting a sport. Are the following statements true or false?

The role of an NGB is to:
a organise match fixing
b organise competitions and events
c appoint managers of professional teams
d organise and provide structure for coaching awards
e encourage gamesmanship
f promote and develop participation in their sport
g enforce the rules and laws of their sport
h promote negative role models
i negotiate TV/sponsorship deals
j build new sport facilities.

Typical mistake

Do not use examples of grassroots organisations if a question asks you about the role of an NGB in developing sport at elite level. Make sure you link points on areas such as coaching and facilities to the higher levels.

Exam checklist

In this section of the course you learned about the roles of National Governing Bodies (NGBs) and what they do for their sport(s). These roles and the functions they fulfil include:

+ promoting participation through schemes, media coverage and equal opportunities
+ developing the sport's coaching and officiating infrastructure and the levels/structure they operate within
+ organising tournaments and competitions, with current examples of these
+ amending the existing rules and applying disciplinary procedures for rule breaking
+ ensuring safety within their sport
+ providing support, insurance and technical guidance to members
+ developing policies and initiatives
+ lobbying for and generating funding.

Check your understanding and progress at www.hoddereducation.co.uk/myrevisionnotes

Exam-style questions

1. Which of the following is not a National Governing Body (NGB) of Sport? [1]
   a England Netball
   b Sport England
   c England Boxing
   d Badminton England

2. Which of the following is not a role of an NGB? [1]
   a Distribute funds throughout a sport
   b Promote participation
   c Organise league and competitions
   d Build facilities for local sports clubs

3. Which of the following is an NGB policy? [1]
   a Issuing officiating awards
   b Training coaches
   c Setting rules of Performance Enhancing Drugs
   d Providing insurance for players

4. Identify three sources of funding available to an NGB which they could use to finance their sport (e.g. the development of new facilities). [3]

5. Identify four ways in which NGBs can support the development of sport locally (i.e. within a community). [4]

6. Using examples, outline two ways in which NGBs can help to provide technical support to clubs. [2]

7. Outline the role of an NGB in developing sport at elite level. [3]

8. State four ways an NGB can promote a sport. [4]

9. A local hockey club is planning to build new changing rooms and a club house, and to upgrade its existing artificial pitch.
   Identify two ways an NGB can help the hockey club. [2]

10. Give three types of advice that an NGB could give to a local community sports club. [3]

11. NGBs have a number of important functions including ensuring safety in their sport and giving their members advice and support (e.g. on insurance).
    Using examples, identify three other roles of NGBs in sport. [6]

12. Using examples, outline and explain the role of National Governing Bodies in generating and distributing funds in the UK. [8]

Topic area 5: The use of technology in sport

5.1 The role of technology in sport

REVISED

5.1.1 To enhance performance

Modern technology has impacted how people can perform in sport. It has allowed sports performers to achieve marginal gains at all levels, from the keen amateur through to elite level sport. It has done this in a variety of different ways.

Accessibility

'Technology' and 'innovation' are key words for those who work in the world of adapted sports equipment, and new designs have increased access to sport for people of all abilities. In the twenty-first century, mobility limitations resulting from disabilities no longer need be barriers to participation in sport and physical activity, at all levels of performance.

Assistive technology in sport is an area of technology where demand for new designs is increasing. New devices are being created to help sports enthusiasts with disabilities to participate at a recreational level, as well as to provide highly advanced equipment for elite Paralympians. Assistive or adapted sports equipment can enable training and exercise to take place, as well as providing the opportunity for participation in sport. For example:
- in athletics, assistive/adaptive equipment is used on the track (e.g. wheelchairs) and in the field (e.g. throwing frames for the shot put and discus)
- lightweight wheelchairs are available for basketball, tennis and road racing
- cross-country sit skis are available, which allow skiers to sit down and push themselves along a set course.

> **Marginal gains** Small improvements to performance (which can often be the difference between winning and losing at elite level).
>
> **Innovation** A new method, idea or product.
>
> **Adapted sports equipment** Any equipment that has been modified to accommodate people with physical differences or disabilities.
>
> **Assistive technology** Products that support and assist people with disabilities or restricted mobility to perform functions they would not otherwise be able to.

Wheelchairs are an important assistive technology in sport and can now be individually designed and adapted to meet the specific requirements of different sports. For example:
- sports such as tennis and basketball require wheelchairs with lightweight frames to enable fast-paced movements, sharp turns and lots of agility at high levels of performance
- contact sports like rugby require wheelchairs with strong reinforced frames and impact/foot protection
- racing wheelchairs are designed with bucket seats, angled wheels for improved stability and a t-frame with a third wheel in front, allowing for precision steering as well as improving balance when moving at speed (e.g. athletics track events such as the 400 m / 800 m).

Figure 5.1 Seated cross-country skier

Simulated environments

Modern technology has helped to improve elite performance by providing simulated competitive environments. Examples include:
+ a simulated bobsleigh run for Winter Olympians and a surf simulator for summer Olympians
+ a hypoxic chamber providing simulated altitude training for endurance athletes
+ 5G and 6G artificial synthetic grass pitches, which can be used whatever the weather all year round, improving access to facilities for sports like football and rugby
+ oxygen tents, which have enabled people to recover more quickly from injury and rehabilitation, getting elite performers back 'on track' as soon as possible.

> **Hypoxic chamber** A sealed room in which the oxygen content of the air is reduced to simulate being at altitude.
>
> **Oxygen tents** An enclosure within which the air supply can be enriched with oxygen to aid a patient's breathing.
>
> **Prosthetic** An artificial body part, such as a limb.

Now test yourself — TESTED

Research how technology has been used to achieve the marginal gains often necessary to succeed at the top level of sport. Draw a spider diagram of methods used to make small improvements in your chosen sport. For example, for cycling you could visit the website for The Science of Sport, at:

https://sportsscientists.com/2017/03/sports-science-marginal-gains-common-sense/

Equipment and clothing

There have also been technological advances in equipment, aiding performance for elite level athletes and other athletes with disabilities. Some examples include:
+ carbon fibre prosthetic devices and lightweight wheelchairs, as mentioned above, which have enabled increased mobility in sports such as athletics and tennis
+ specially tailored running shoes, which have been designed by companies such as Nike and ASICS to improve elite marathon performance
+ track shoes, which have become lighter and better at providing grip for cornering helping to improve performance at all levels
+ footballs, which are now designed to allow more swing and curve
+ lighter golf clubs, which increase swing speeds and enable performers to hit golf balls further and with more control
+ lighter, better ventilated and more affordable cricket helmets
+ smaller turbo engines in Formula 1 cars, which are more fuel efficient.

Technological advances in sport clothing have led to:
+ lighter, more aerodynamic body wear for sports such as cycling, ensuring no extra restrictions are placed on the performer (e.g. a skinsuit is designed to be the most aerodynamic clothing you can wear; premium skinsuits feature special fabrics designed to reduce drag and manipulate airflow)
+ improved comfort when performing as a result of moisture-wicking fabric – a kind of fabric that is commonly used in workout clothing and sportswear because the material is designed to pull moisture (e.g. sweat/perspiration) away from the skin and out to the exterior of the fabric.

Monitoring of exercise

Technology enables the highly accurate monitoring of exercise rates and physiological responses to performance. Examples include:
+ wearable devices, which are used to track the heart rates of performers
+ lab-based testing, which is used to identify the strengths and weaknesses of a performer and then monitor their progress and assess the effectiveness of their training programmes (e.g. via GPS)
+ GPS software tracking systems, which help coaches to monitor players during matches as well as in training – these systems give coaches a vast amount of information at the touch of a button, tracking the speed, distance and direction of the individuals; GPS technology has recently entered the world of football and many believe it will become increasingly popular in the coming years
+ video/DVD/digital technology, which is increasingly being used by coaches and athletes to analyse individual technique as well as team performances (e.g. individual technique in field athletic events such as shot, discus and javelin; and team performances in relation to roles at set plays, e.g. zonal marking by a football team at a corner).

> **Aerodynamic** Having a shape that reduces the drag from air moving past.
>
> **GPS (Global Positioning System)** A space-based navigation system that provides information about location and time.
>
> **Gait analysis** An evaluation of someone's style of walking or running.

> **Check your understanding**
>
> 1 Identify two ways in which assistive technology is being used in the sport of athletics.
> 2 Give one sporting example for each of the following ways technology can enhance performance:
>   a Accessibility
>   b Simulated environments
>   c Equipment
>   d Clothing
>   e Monitoring

5.1.2 To increase the safety of participants

Technology has helped make training and performance safer and decreased injury risks to elite athletes. Some examples are given in Table 5.1.

Table 5.1 Examples of technology that have helped to make sport safer

Technology	How it has increased the safety of participants
3D laboratory-based gait analysis	Helps to identify errors in running styles, which can then be adapted to help prevent injury
Video analysis	Used to analyse biomechanical aspects of performance; information gained is also potentially helpful in injury rehabilitation (e.g. an in-depth breakdown of the way a long distance athlete runs)
Wearable hydration devices	Used to inform performers about their hydration levels to avoid the potential negative impacts of dehydration
Respiratory monitoring	Used to monitor an athlete's heart rate, respiratory rates and any irregularity in breathing to inform their exercise (e.g. Strados monitoring)

Technology has also improved:
+ protective equipment for sports performers in high contact or high speed sports (e.g. helmets for cricket, ice hockey and cycling)
+ gloves for golf and football
+ protective padding and guards for boxing, hockey and football
+ mouth guards for rugby union and hockey
+ halo head protection in Formula 1.

The ability to rest and recover from the demands of intense training and competition is sometimes neglected when considering elite performance. However, technology has been developed to improve sleep, enabling appropriate rest and recovery from training or competition; sleep is important for physiological recovery as well as an individual's reaction time. Players at some professional clubs (e.g. in football) who are poor sleepers are given wrist bands (e.g. Fatigue Science Readiband), which use movement sensors to assess sleep quality.

> **Now test yourself** — TESTED
>
> Using the link below, or an alternative website of your choice, research how oxygen tents can help athletes recover from injury.
>
> https://www.omstc.org/ocsi/

> **Now test yourself** — TESTED
>
> Research ways in which technology can be used to improve performer safety. For example, the article from BizTech Magazine linked below discusses the application of technology to improve safe practice in sports such as football and hockey:
>
> https://biztechmagazine.com/article/2018/10/new-technology-strives-make-sports-safer-players

> **Exam tip**
>
> To gain the most marks in your exam, it is important to be able to link technology that enhances the safety of participants to named sporting activities.

> **Typical mistake**
>
> Be careful not to lose marks by writing about something that does not answer the question (e.g. if the focus of the question is *performers*, don't write about advantages of technology to *spectators*).

> **Check your understanding**
>
> 3 List three examples of sporting technology that increases the safety of participants.

5.1.3 To increase fair play and increase the accuracy of officiating

Technology can make sport fairer – by helping to catch cheats – and more inclusive. It helps officials to make more reliable and accurate decisions (e.g. via instant replays and reviews of decisions in sports such as tennis, football and rugby), which increases trust in them. Improved communications (e.g. via microphone) allow officials to consult with one another and instantly relay opinions to a referee or umpire. Spectators are often able to watch a big screen or TV replay to keep them informed and entertained while awaiting decisions.

Examples of the technology that officials use to help ensure fair outcomes and accurate decisions are outlined in Table 5.2.

Table 5.2 How officials use technology to make sport 'fairer'

Areas in which technology is used	Explanation	Examples
Officiating	Technology helps officials to make fairer, reliable and accurate decisions during play	In football, the video assistant referee (VAR) in football checks off-sides and hand balls
		In cricket, officiating technology has increased fairness via the use of:
		the Third Umpire (who reviews TV replays, and technology including Hawkeye, the Snick-O-Meter, Hot Spot [which determines if the ball has hit the bat] and the camera to determine no balls at the crease, and gives advice to the main umpire on disputed catches, boundaries, run outs, etc.)
		the Decision Review System (DRS) which allows team captains to challenge decisions made by on-field umpires with up to three unsuccessful appeals per innings
		Tennis officials use Hawkeye to check if a ball was in or out of court dimensions
Measurement/better timing devices	Technology provides more accurate measuring devices and more accurate timing systems	In track events, technology is used to measure times and distances, and for making decisions at the finish line
		Technology is used to judge which athlete, cyclist, etc. finished in which place
		Athletic events use laser technology to judge the height of jumps and the distance of throws more accurately
		Technology is used to keep time accurately, including stoppage time (e.g. the shot clock in basketball to speed up play and increase excitement)
Overturning decisions	Technology is used to reverse decisions that have been found to be incorrect	VAR technology is used in football to reverse decisions about penalties and off-sides
		The leg before wicket (LBW) technology in cricket, via ball tracking, is used to make decisions about whether a player is out
Reduction in cheating	Technology is used to improve detection of foul play and/or gamesmanship, sometimes via retrospective (i.e. post-event) disciplinary action and a panel to review incidents that a match official might have missed	Playback facilities, which enable officials to watch on-field events from different angles, allow for confirmation of whether a foul or violation has been committed (e.g. rugby union/rugby league 'on report' system)
		Technology allows for confirmation of whether there has been a false start (e.g. in athletics 100 m sprinting, motor sensors built into starting blocks detect if an athlete moves within 0.01 seconds of the gun being fired; if they do, the athlete has false started and is eliminated from the race under current rules)
Drug testing	Increased investment in technology is used to improve the detection of doping	e.g. through the use of athlete biological passports
Inclusion	Technology allows for the inclusion of athletes with disabilities	e.g. via adaptive equipment

> **Exam tip**
>
> If a question asks you to discuss the impact of officiating technology on fairness in sport, you must provide answers that outline the positive impact as well as the negative.

> **Typical mistake**
>
> If a student answered a 'Discuss' question on officiating technology (e.g. goal line technology, also known as the goal decision system (GDS) in football) by only writing about the positive impact of such technology and did not cover the negatives as well, they would lose marks.

> **Now test yourself** TESTED
>
> Follow the link below to read an article debating the use of technology by officials in rugby union.
>
> https://www.rugbydump.com/news/referees-and-technology-better-decision-making/
>
> Note down the positives and negatives of officiating technology that you read about, or see in the supporting video clips.

> **Check your understanding**
>
> 4. What do the acronyms stand for in the following examples of officiating technology?
>   a. VAR
>   b. TMO
>   c. DRS
>   d. GDS
> 5. Identify three ways in which the use of officiating technology in cricket has helped make the sport fairer.

5.1.4 To enhance spectatorship

Watching sport is no longer a purely passive experience, whether you are watching at home or live in a ground or stadium such as Wembley or Wimbledon. Technology has enhanced spectators' experience of watching sport in a number of ways including the following:

+ **Camera coverage:** remote controlled micro-cameras provide more angles, track individual athletes or provide a performer's view point to keep fans fully involved and engaged in what they are watching.
+ **Statistical information:** an individual or team's match play/past performances are available on screen or at the click of a button during play, which keeps fans well informed about both the sport and the performers (e.g. Prozone is used to analyse Premier League football and footballers).
+ **Interactive software:** apps offer access to sporting information, competitions, games and votes via links on tickets and programmes or via downloads.
+ **Screens in stadia:** to allow spectators to view appeals made by players.

> **Prozone** A new computerised video system that allows the tracking of many individuals performing a sporting activity, such as football. It can be accessed by performance analysts as well as fans of individual clubs.

> **Check your understanding**
>
> 6. How has camera coverage helped enhance spectatorship?

5.2 Positive and negative effects of the use of technology in sport

REVISED

5.2.1 Positive effects

Enhanced performance

We discussed how GPS can aid elite performer development in the previous section, but it can also benefit athletes at all levels. Strava is just one example of how both elite and non-elite athletes can improve their performance via GPS technologies that are becoming more readily available.

GPS tracking apps – on smartphones or dedicated GPS devices – bring together athletes from all over the world who are working hard and determined to achieve their best. It helps people to connect, compare and compete with one another, lets individuals track their swims, rides and runs, and helps them to analyse and quantify their performance, and to use the data to provide the motivation to improve their performance.

Lower risk of injury and quicker recovery from injury

Technology can help to lower the risk of injury and speed up the recovery process. These kinds of technology include **vibration therapy**, which has a number of possible health benefits. It:

+ improves bone density, increases muscle power and improves circulation
+ reduces joint pain and/or delays onset of muscle soreness
+ alleviates stress
+ boosts metabolism
+ maintains cartilage integrity where weight-bearing activities are difficult to undertake.

Electrostimulation uses electrical impulses to contract the muscles. It can help to prevent injury and speed up recovery time by:

+ strengthening muscles
+ helping to prevent a loss of fitness by maintaining muscle tone during periods of inactivity (via application to specific muscle groups)
+ assisting in rehabilitation through the gradual strengthening of injured or weakened muscles
+ helping to get rid of lactic acid after a training session or competition, as well as decreasing muscle tension/potential injury by relaxing the muscles.

> **Vibration therapy** Also known as 'whole body vibration' (WBV), can involve the use of vibration plates to induce the effects of exercise in the body.
>
> **Electrostimulation** The administration of electric current in specified doses to organs or systems of an organism in order to stimulate the action of the organs or systems.

More accurate decisions

Modern technology has made decision-making more accurate, for example:

+ multiple camera angles – every aspect of a sporting performance or contest can be reviewed (e.g. officiating decisions such as tight off-sides)
+ slow-motion action replays/playback technology – via giant screens at an event or by clicking a button at home to rewind live action and view a slowed down replay of what has just happened.

> **Now test yourself** TESTED
>
> Hawkeye is an example of technology that is widely used in officiating to aid the decision-making process. Research Hawkeye technology and write a sentence on how it is used in three sports of your choice (e.g. cricket, tennis and football).

Technical analysis

Modern technology has also improved technical analysis by providing the viewer with a greater insight into and understanding of a sport or sporting event.

Experts are increasingly being asked to review and analyse performance in fine detail (e.g. via motion capture analysis). These experts are known as pundits.

5.2.2 Negative effects

Increased cost
+ Technology can be expensive and unaffordable for some, leading to potential inequalities and/or unfair advantages if the technology is not available to all.
+ Decreased live attendances lead to lower sporting revenues if individuals choose the 'cheaper option' of following an event on TV or via the radio or internet.

Unequal access and affordability
+ Technology creates inequality as some cannot afford the new technologies being developed (e.g. poorer nations).
+ In addition to cost, access to modern technology may be limited in some sports/locations and therefore not available at all levels of competition.

Reduction in flow of the game
+ The introduction of officiating technology can cause long delays or disruption, and a potential reduction in the flow of the game. This could negatively impact on the performer (e.g. while awaiting the review decision of an official).
+ The use of video playbacks and delays in decision-making can sometimes irritate spectators.

Influence on officials' decisions
Modern technology influences official's decisions, but cannot make decisions or apply the best interpretation of the rules. This can lead to:
+ increased pressure on officials, due to the exposure and constant media scrutiny of their decisions
+ lack of trust in the decisions made by officials, which can undermine the respect we have for them.

> **Motion capture analysis** The process of recording and then analysing the movement of objects or people.
>
> **Pundit/punditry** A knowledgeable person who, via the media, offers their opinion, guidance or commentary on a particular sport.

> **Typical mistake**
> It may be tempting to focus on a particular negative or positive impact of technology on sport. Do not forget to learn both the positive and negative effects of the use of any technology.

> **Exam tip**
> In extended questions in particular, make sure that when the command word 'explain' is used, you include the additional level of detail required to fully develop your answer and achieve the highest marks.

> **Check your understanding**
> 7 Why might cost be an issue with technology in relation to a sports performer?

5.2.3 Positive and negative effects of technology on the spectator experience

Technology has changed the way spectators interact with sport in a variety of ways. Table 5.3 summarises how various technological advancements have had both positive and negative effects on spectators.

Table 5.3 Positive and negative effects of technology on spectators

Technology	Positive effect	Negative effect
Big screens in the ground or stadium	Increased sense of crowd excitement/involvement (e.g. awaiting decisions via big screen, Hawkeye) Easier to view participant activities (e.g. in athletics you can view field events and the start and finish of track events from different positions in the stadium)	Screens can cause unexpected spectator chanting or cheering which could be a distraction for performers Screens can distract from the actual play
Media broadcasting	Sport is shown worldwide so fans can see live matches anywhere in the world and support their team Media advancements and satellite technologies make a wider range of sports more accessible to spectators Broadcasters can change the timing of events so fans can access them at prime time Improved experience of watching sport at home (e.g. HD/split-screen coverage)	The media can highlight or feature negative behaviour that occurs both during and away from sport, damaging the reputation of a sport and causing spectators to switch off
Pause/live TV replays	Instant replays can be used to help see what has happened in order to help spectators understand the decisions reached	Spectators can see the action and analyse each movement which can cause arguments/trouble between fans over a bad tackle or aggressive behaviour Replays could lead to spectators questioning refereeing decisions
Video assistant referee (VAR)	Spectators can also review play to help understand the decisions reached	Time spent reaching decisions interrupts the flow of the game Sometimes decisions reached are highly controversial, particularly in relation to offences such as off-side and handball
Technology providing statistical information on sport	Tracking player movement provides increased understanding on player and team performance, e.g.: time in possession number of successful/unsuccessful passes shots on target goals/baskets scored number of assists made	Information on players' performance can lead to criticism of the team and/or player performance
Television match official (TMO)	Increased proportion of accurate decisions/increased fairness Increased entertainment due to tension/drama as spectators await decisions/replays occur Increased accountability of officials in elite level/professional sport where sporting results have significant financial implications Fairer sporting outcomes Increased expert debate for audiences to listen to	Slows game down; can mean prolonged interruptions in play Increased certainty of decision-making may make sport less entertaining for some The crowd may influence outcomes if giant screens in the stadium show replays TV producers' choice of replays might affect officiating (or the third official on the touchline if there is access to replay before a restart) Human error is still not eliminated – decisions may still be wrong or inconclusive Only available at highest levels of professional sport

Check your understanding and progress at www.hoddereducation.co.uk/myrevisionnotes

> **Exam tip**
>
> Make sure you can evaluate the impact of technology on spectators.

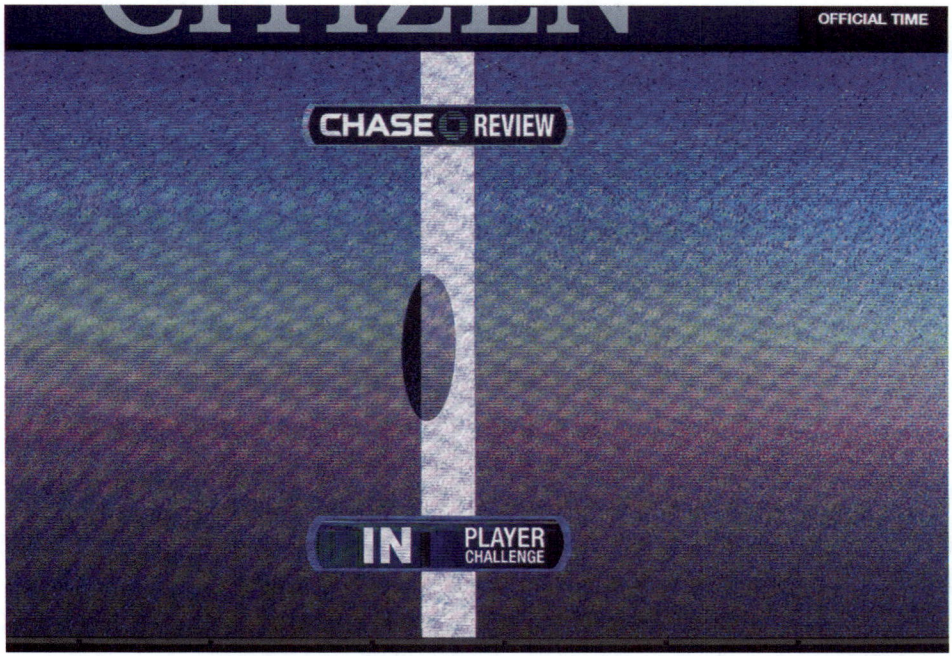

Figure 5.2 Hawkeye technology in tennis

> **Now test yourself** TESTED ○
>
> In addition to helping officials reach the correct decisions, Hawkeye has a number of other potential uses in sport. Describe how Hawkeye can be used to enhance the *spectator experience*.

> **Check your understanding**
>
> 8 How have sports spectators benefited from advancements in technology?
> 9 What are the negative effects of video assistant referees (VAR) in Premier League football?
> 10 What meaningful statistical information could technology provide on sports performers, which could be of interest to fans of sports such as football, rugby, basketball and netball?
> 11 Discuss whether the use of television match officials (TMO) in sport has been positive or negative for spectators.

> **Exam checklist**
>
> In this section you learned about the use of technology in sport, including:
> + the role of technology in enhancing performance, lowering the risk of injury and speeding up recovery from injury, and increasing the accuracy of officiating and technical analysis
> + the positive and negative effects of the use of technology in sport on performers, officials and spectators.

Exam-style questions

1. Which of the following is a *negative* aspect of technology when used to aid officials in their decision-making? [1]
   a Increased performer confidence in the correct decisions being made
   b Increased disruption to a sporting event as a result of excessive referee referrals
   c Increased excitement in the crowd as decisions are awaited on the big screen
   d Increased accuracy of timings or measurements taken

2. Which of the following is *not* an example of officiating technology? [1]
   a TMO
   b VAR
   c GDS
   d EIS

3. Which of the following is *not* a potential negative impact of technology on a sports performer? [1]
   a High costs of technology
   b Lack of access to technology
   c Use of technology to mask an injury
   d Use of technology to aid training programmes

4. Define the term 'electrostimulation'. [1]

5. Identify two negative impacts of technology for a sports performer. [2]

6. Identify three examples of sporting technology that has changed the way spectators interact with sport. [3]

7. Using examples, state four positive effects of sporting technology that have changed the way spectators interact with sport. [4]

8. How can vibration therapy lower the risk of injury and speed up recovery time in sports performers? [3]

9. Outline the negative effects of the increased use of technology to help officials in their decision-making. [3]

10. Identify how the increased use of technology to aid officials in their decision-making has improved porting events. [4]

11. Why might some fans be against the use of goal-line technology and others be in favour of its introduction? [4]

12. Discuss whether modern technology has made sport fairer. [8]

Check your understanding and progress at www.hoddereducation.co.uk/myrevisionnotes

Answers to 'Check your understanding' questions

Topic area 1

1. Elderly parents; siblings; relatives
2. Physical and sensory disabilities, or those with a mental health condition
3. Unemployment affects disposable income so individuals may not be able to afford the costs of participation; it can also affect levels of motivation.
4. Lack of transport
5. Appropriate pricing for all user groups (e.g. concessions, taster sessions and free or reduced-price equipment).
6. Lack of appropriate activity provision (e.g. due to existing stereotypes) mean that women may not be able to access the sports/activities they wish to participate in (e.g. if they are not seen as 'female appropriate' activities as in the case of boxing and weightlifting, which require aggression and power – often seen as stereotypically 'male' characteristics).
7. Providing activities/sessions at various times to meet the needs of different user groups including carers; providing respite care to free up some time for activity for young carers.
8. Planning physical activity to fit in with busy daily lifestyles (e.g. 10 minute HIIT sessions); providing access to facilities/activities at times to suit people who work.
9. Climate can be a negative influence on the popularity of cricket in the UK because even in a shortened 'summer' season, frequent interruptions to play due to bad weather can lead to a loss of interest.
10. Free-to-air coverage of a sport and access to it live and on catch-up via a terrestrial TV station or via radio gives access to a far bigger audience than if a sport is only shown on subscription channels.
11. Due to it being perceived as violent with the potential to cause injury (e.g. to the head) to the participants during the normal course of competition, as the sport involves punching an opponent.
12. Examples include: netball, basketball, rounders, athletics and swimming.
13. Futsal matches are shorter, so it can be played in reduced time-periods, which suits the lifestyle of some participants (e.g. working people).

Topic area 2

1. Seven values which can be promoted through sport:
   + Team spirit
   + Fair play
   + Citizenship
   + Tolerance AND respect
   + Inclusion
   + National pride
   + Excellence
2. People giving up their time to act as volunteers/sports coaches and helping to run local community sports clubs
3. Accepting and welcoming players from different social backgrounds and gaining a greater understanding of different cultures
4. The closeness between the five continents of the world
5. Excellence, friendship and respect
6. Inspiration, determination, courage and equality
7. Via the idea of struggle and redefining the boundaries of possibility
8. Through its fight against discrimination for everyone who plays, watches or works in football
9. 'This Girl Can'; 'Chance to Shine'; 'Football for Hope', Rainbow Laces, Sporting Equals
10. The unwritten rules concerning player behaviour
11. The rules or guidelines for spectators at a sporting event
12. Reasons why observing etiquette is important for a sports performer:
    + ensures fairness/a fair result is achieved
    + promotes and reinforces positive values (e.g. respect for others)
    + helps to ensure the safety of themselves and their opponents
    + sets a good example to young people and provides an example of a positive role model to children
    + improves the reputation of the sport and encourages participation in the sport (e.g. rugby union)
    + ensures an activity or game can be played effectively in a free-flowing and enjoyable manner
    + as an elite or professional performer, it might help gain sponsorship deals.

13 Any three from:
- a tennis player is about to serve at Wimbledon
- a golfer is about to putt at The Open Championship
- a snooker player is about to take a shot
- a rugby player is about to take a conversion
- a diver is preparing to dive.

14 a gamesmanship
   b sportsmanship
   c gamesmanship
   d gamesmanship
   e gamesmanship

15 Examples include: maintaining silence when a player is about to putt or take a shot; a player acknowledging or applauding an opponent's shot (e.g. a good bunker shot from a difficult position or a hole in one)

16 World Anti-Doping Agency

17 UK Anti-Doping Agency (UKAD)

Topic area 3

1 A regular event is held each year but in a different city each time (e.g. the UEFA Champions League Final).
   A one-off event is held in a host city once in a generation (e.g. the Olympics).
   A regular and recurring event is held once a year in the same venue each year (e.g. the Wimbledon Tennis Championships).

2 a False – it is held every year in a different city each time.
   b True
   c True
   d False – this event must be linked to the word 'Final'.
   e True

3 Any three from:
   - Olympic Games
   - Paralympic Games
   - Netball World Cup
   - Formula 1 Grand Prix races
   - Commonwealth Games
   - African Cup of Nations
   - Asian Games.

4 i – b
   ii – a
   iii – e
   iv – c
   v – d

5 Bids likely include plans for building new sports facilities, which could increase participation in sport at a grassroots level, as well as providing facilities for elite performers who require specialist centres to train and compete in.

6 Any answer including the lack of public support due to the very high cost involved in bidding for and hosting events, including development of venues and infrastructure/transport.

7 Direct tourism is where people visit the host city or country because they are attending a major sporting event *as it happens*. Indirect tourism is where people visit the host city or country *after an event*, having been made aware of it as a result of global media coverage.

8 Poor performance by the home nation or team can have a negative impact on national pride/morale.

9 There may be a loss in national reputation or status if the event was badly organised, the host nation's participants performed badly or scandals emerged.

10 Potential long-term drawbacks of hosting could include:
   - financial problems; hosts cannot cover very high costs
   - negative legacy of unused sporting facilities
   - a loss of national reputation if the event goes badly.

Topic area 4

1 Independent, self-appointed organisations that govern their sports through the common consent of their sport

2 - Surfing England
   - England Boxing
   - England Handball
   - Badminton England
   - British Cycling
   - Rounders England

3 Any six NGBs not listed in question 2 above, including:
   - Football Association
   - Rugby Football Union
   - England Netball

4 - The Racket Pack (for ages 5–11)
   - SmashUp! (for ages 11–16)

5 Strategies include:
   + using/involving themselves in promotional campaigns (e.g. 'This Girl Can')
   + providing equal access to sports facilities (e.g. via equal opportunities policies)
   + providing taster sessions/women-only sessions in sports such as boxing
   + ensuring media coverage promotes female role models
   + training and developing more female sports coaches and officials in their sport.
6 + Into Officiating Course
   + C Award Umpire Course
   + B Award Umpire Course
   + A Award Umpire Course
7 + Foundation Award in Coaching Badminton
   + Coach Award in Coaching Badminton
   + UKCC Level 3 Certificate for Head Coach in Badminton
8 Any four from:
   + National Cadet and Junior League (aimed at grassroots players)
   + Team and individual competitions for schools
   + English Leagues Cup Competitions
   + County Championships
   + Inter-Regionals
   + Grand Prix events
   + British League
   + National Championships
   + 1*–4* competitions.
9 A coach; a volunteer; a player; a manager; the club itself; the chairman/chairwoman of a club; a club official such as the secretary/treasurer
10 Any two from:
   + providing a dedicated area on their website for legal advice, guidelines and information
   + assistance with facility development
   + advice on equipment, venues and surfaces
   + location and contact details for local clubs and advice on how to get started/involved in the sport
   + support for the development of a sport locally and at elite level via provision.
11 The process by which an athlete can obtain official approval to use a prescribed prohibited substance or method for the treatment of a legitimate medical condition
12 Any six from:
   + lobby for and receive funding
   + Sport England
   + grants/government funding
   + membership/national affiliation fees
   + subscription/match fees
   + National Lottery funding/UK Sport
   + media/TV rights
   + income from sponsorship/advertising
   + donations
   + merchandising
   + admission charges/ticket sales
   + NGB initiatives.
13 a False
   b True
   c True
   d True
   e False
   f True
   g True
   h False
   i True
   j False

Topic area 5

1 Lightweight wheelchairs for track and road racing; throwing frames for shot put and discus
2 a Accessibility – any one from:
   – lightweight wheelchairs for basketball, tennis and road racing
   – cross-country sit skis, which allow skiers to sit down and push themselves along a set course.
  b Simulated environments – any one from:
   – a simulated bobsleigh run
   – a surf simulator
   – hypoxic chambers
   – 5G and 6G artificial synthetic grass pitches
   – oxygen tents.
  c Equipment – any one from:
   – carbon fibre prosthetic devices
   – lightweight wheelchairs
   – specially tailored running shoes
   – lighter track shoes with better grip
   – footballs designed to allow more swing and curve
   – lighter golf clubs to increase swing speeds in order to hit golf balls further and with more control
   – lighter, better ventilated and more affordable cricket helmets
   – smaller turbo engines in Formula 1 cars.
  d Clothing – any one from:
   – lighter, more aerodynamic body wear
   – moisture wicking fabric.
  e Monitoring – any one from:
   – wearable tracking devices
   – lab-based testing
   – GPS software tracking systems
   – video/DVD/digital technology.

3 Any three from:
  - 3D laboratory-based gait analysis
  - video analysis, which can be used to analyse biomechanical aspects of performance
  - improved protective equipment for sports performers in high contact sports
  - gloves for golf and football
  - protective padding and guards for boxing, hockey and football
  - mouth guards for rugby union and hockey
  - halo head protection in Formula 1.

4 a video assistant referee
  b television match official
  c decision review system
  d goal detection system (i.e. Goal Ref)

5 Technology in cricket has made sport fairer via:
  - the Third Umpire (who offers advice to the main umpire on disputed catches, boundaries, run outs, etc.)
  - the DRS, which gives team captains the right to challenge decisions made by on-field umpires with up to three unsuccessful appeals per innings
  - examples of TV technology also used by the Third Umpire: Hawkeye, Snick-O-Meter, Hot Spot and no balls at the crease.

6 Camera coverage enhances spectatorship by:
  - providing more angles via remote controlled micro-cameras
  - tracking individual athletes
  - providing a performer's view point to keep fans fully involved and engaged in what they are watching.

7 The high costs of technology mean that performers may not be able to afford it. This leads to issues with availability – elite level performers may not all have access to the same level of technology, so some cannot use it to aid/improve their performance. This could create inequalities between those who can afford it/access it and those who can't.

8 Benefits include:
  - increased crowd excitement/sense of involvement (e.g. when awaiting decisions via big screen or watching Hawkeye)
  - improved experience of watching sport at home (e.g. HD/split-screen coverage)
  - increased excitement from watching improved performances resulting from technological advancements
  - a wider range of sports are more accessible as a result of media advancements and satellite technologies.

9 Negative effects of VAR include:
  - time spent reaching decisions can interrupt the flow of the game
  - some decisions can be highly controversial, particularly in relation to offences such as off-side and handball.

10 Technology can provide information on:
  - player movement patterns (by tracking)
  - time in possession
  - number of successful/unsuccessful passes
  - shots on target
  - goals/baskets scored
  - number of assists made.

11 Positive/for TMOs:
  - increased proportion of accurate decisions/increased fairness
  - increased entertainment due to tension/drama as spectators wait for decisions or replays to occur
  - increased accountability of officials in elite level/professional sport where results have significant financial implications
  - fairer sporting outcomes
  - increased expert debate for audiences to listen to.

Negative/against TMOs:
  - slows game down/can lead to prolonged interruptions in play
  - increased certainty of decision-making may make sport less entertaining for some
  - the crowd may influence outcomes if giant screens in stadiums show replays
  - TV producers' choice of replays might affect officiating (and third official on touchline if there is access to replays before a restart)
  - human error is still not eliminated – decisions may still be wrong/inconclusive; TMOs are only available at highest levels/professional sport.

Answers to exam-style questions

Topic area 1

1. a Any three from:
    - lack of time
    - lack of disposable income/costs are too high
    - lack of (female) role models for single parents
    - family commitments
    - lack of childcare availability
    - lack of awareness (e.g. of activities/facilities available to them)
    - lack of activities to join in with together
    - lack of motivation/lack of self-esteem.

   b Any relevant example particularly suited to single parents with a lack of time/funds/childcare, e.g. Ultimate Frisbee.

2. a Any four from:
    - lack of (adapted) transport
    - lack of access to facilities (e.g. ramps)
    - lack of suitable activity provision
    - lack of appropriate equipment (e.g. hoists)
    - lack of trained staff
    - lack of awareness of provision/activities on offer
    - lack of self-esteem
    - possible lack of disposable income.

   b Total 4 marks (1 mark for each way and 1 for each linked example):
    - Specialist equipment (e.g. hoists into swimming pools)
    - Improved access to buildings (e.g. wheelchair ramps)
    - Provide adapted transport to pools (e.g. minibus/taxi with lifts/wheelchair access)
    - Advertise/targeted promotion to people with disabilities (e.g. information in a variety of formats, such as braille)
    - User-specific sessions (e.g. swimming sessions only for people with disabilities/provision of specialist coaches).

3. Total 4 marks (1 mark for each barrier and 1 for each linked solution)
   - Lack of time – fit in activities at school (e.g. at lunch time or after school)
   - Lack of own transport/reliance on others for lifts – organise transport (e.g. with friends/family members)
   - Lack of positive role models/parental encouragement – use positive role models pupils can relate to; educate parents on the benefits of physical activity for their teenage children
   - Lack of interest/motivation – promote the health benefits of activity; provide activities that appeal to teenagers (e.g. skateboarding, parkour, etc.).

4. Total 4 marks (1 mark for each factor and 1 for each linked description)

Factor	Description
Provision/access/facilities	Increased participation if good local availability; the reverse is true if not
Positive role models/national success at swimming	Medal success at events like the Olympics can inspire participation
Social acceptability	Swimming is viewed as an important life skill
Available in school curriculum	Increased popularity if taught in schools (e.g. as part of the National Curriculum PE)
Environment	Increased participation if you live close to the sea

5. a Any three from:
    - lack of disposable income/money/the expense of equipment
    - lack of own transport
    - lack of time due to exams/part-time work
    - lack of awareness of activity provision
    - lack of role models
    - poor body image; low self-esteem
    - lack of motivation.

   b Any two from:
    - subsidise activities for teenagers; give them price concessions
    - arrange transport with family members/friends
    - provide alternative/flexible session programming (e.g. at weekends)
    - increase promotion/advertising of what is available to increase awareness
    - provide single-sex/same-gender sessions
    - offer appealing activity options.

6. a i Can't afford it due to high costs (e.g. equipment/membership fees)

    ii Lack of clubs/awareness of sessions suitable for older people; lack of tennis courts/facilities in their local area/lack of transport

   b i Subsidise sessions/equipment/membership costs for older people/people over the age of 60

    ii Set up more clubs, provide sessions aimed at older people or provide transport to existing clubs/facilities

Answers to exam-style questions

7 1 mark each for:
   + gender
   + people with family commitments
   + parents (single)
   + people who work.

8 a Any two from:
   - retired people/people over the age of 60
   - unemployed people
   - older teenagers (e.g. those who have left full-time education).

   b Any two from:
   - school children
   - teenagers in full-time education
   - families with young children
   - people with family commitments
   - employed/working singles/couples.

9 b

10 Total 2 marks (1 mark for each reason and linked example)

   Some sports have a short season because the weather can limit the opportunities to play/watch them (e.g. cricket).

   The local climate means that some activities are only available in some areas of the UK and at limited times (e.g. snow sports such as skiing/snowboarding).

11 a Environment/climate not suitable (lack of snow); lack of provision of artificial ski slopes in some areas; lack of elite performer success/role models to inspire participation; high costs/expense (e.g. of equipment/facility hire)

   b Social acceptability (e.g. if viewed as a violent sport with risk/fear of injury); positive role models/success of elite (Olympic) performers helps build the popularity of the sport; lack of provision (e.g. lack of clubs/specialist facilities in the area you live)

   (Accept reverse points as appropriate)

12 b

13 Any four from:
   + amount of media coverage/advertising
   + level of provision/clubs/number of facilities
   + requirement for specialist equipment
   + cost of participation
   + availability of competitions/leagues
   + access to qualified coaches
   + number of fans
   + image of sport, whether or not it is seen as 'fashionable'
   + attractiveness to sponsors
   + sufficient number of role models.

14 Any two from:
   + lack of awareness/lack of media coverage
   + lack of provision/clubs/facilities
   + (long) distance to travel to nearest club
   + facility/venue is expensive
   + lack of inclusion in school PE programme/National Curriculum PE
   + lack of role models
   + lack of coaches.

15 Use the following indicative content alongside the level of response grids when marking extended (8 mark) questions:

   + **Environment/climate:** lack of snow for winter sports such as snowboarding/skiing may make the sport(s) less popular; cold/wet weather may make cricket less popular while the perfect climate for football and rugby make these sports potentially more popular.

   + **Media coverage/advertising/awareness:** some sports get more exposure in the media than others which increases their popularity (football, tennis, etc. get lots of coverage while hockey, basketball, etc. don't).

   + **Previous success of the sport/sports performers:** the sporting success of individuals/teams/sports will increase popularity in that sport, and the reverse is also true (e.g. sports like cycling have increased in popularity following Tour de France Olympic success).

   + **Strong infrastructure:** giving opportunities to participate/gain participation awards increases the popularity of a sport (e.g. athletics clubs/schemes).

   + **Provision of facilities/activities/sessions:** sports with more provision/accessible provision are more popular (e.g. there are lots of football and rugby pitches compared to fewer swimming pools, which positively and negatively impacts on participation in a sport).

   + **Level of spectatorship:** more opportunities to spectate, both at the event as well as via media outlets such as TV/internet, increases the popularity of some sports (e.g. football, tennis and rugby) but not others with more limited coverage (e.g. basketball, hockey and table tennis).

   + **Role models (or lack of):** positive role models can inspire participation (e.g. Sir Bradley Wiggins, Sir Chris Hoy, Victoria Pendleton and Laura Trott in cycling).

   + **Legacy of previous sporting events:** the London 2012 Olympics helped boost the sport of cycling; 2003 and 2019 World Cup successes in rugby and cricket helped increase participation in these sports.

   + **Tradition (or lack of):** where a sport has been played for a long time it is often more popular (e.g. football, rugby, tennis, etc.).

   + **Inclusivity of the sport:** sports that enable all abilities/genders to participate together may become more popular (e.g. park runs and 10 km road races are good examples of mixed gender opportunities).

   + **Social acceptability:** boxing is less socially acceptable with some (e.g. due to its link to violence/blows to the head).

Check your understanding and progress at www.hoddereducation.co.uk/myrevisionnotes

Topic area 2

1. a False
   b False
   c True
2. Total 3 marks (1 mark for each of the following): National pride, citizenship, inclusion
3. Any three from: Inspiration, Determination, Courage, Equality
4. Total 3 marks (1 mark for each correct match)
   1 – c
   2 – a
   3 – b
5. Any three from:
   + applauding the performance or success of an opponent (e.g. when scoring a goal in football)
   + shaking hands with opponents and officials before and/or after a game
   + showing grace and respect at the end of a game whether you have won or lost
   + showing respect to and freely accepting the decisions of officials
   + returning the ball to the opposition in football when they have kicked it out because of an injury to one of your team.
6. Any two from:
   + ensuring fairness/a fair result is achieved
   + promoting and reinforcing positive values (e.g. respect for others)
   + helping to ensure the safety of themselves and their opponents
   + setting a good example to young people and providing a positive role model to children
   + improving the reputation of the sport and encouraging participation in the sport (e.g. rugby union)
   + ensuring an activity or game can be played effectively in a free flowing and enjoyable manner
   + as an elite or professional performer, it might help gain sponsorship deals.
7. d
8. Any three from:
   + delaying a restart to a contest or 'running down the clock' (i.e. time wasting) when winning
   + over-appealing (e.g. over-complaining in cricket in order to pressure an umpire into making a decision to benefit your team)
   + taking an injury time-out even when not injured (e.g. in cricket or tennis)
   + grunting loudly in tennis when playing a shot in order to put an opponent off.
9. Any three from:
   + being quiet during play (e.g. as a tennis player is about to serve at Wimbledon, or a golfer is about to putt at The Open Championship, or a snooker player is about to take a shot)
   + remaining quiet and standing up when an opposition's national anthem plays in order to show tolerance and respect of different countries through sport
   + respecting and accepting decisions made by officials and not swearing or using aggressive behaviour towards them
   + not making negative comments or directing racist/sexist chants towards other players, supporters or officials
   + not going onto the playing area (e.g. respecting the line in football via 'non-trespass')
   + not displaying aggressive behaviour (e.g. towards officials or the opposition)
   + recognising good performance from both teams (e.g. applauding an opponent's skill or goal)
   + observing the safety of players (e.g. not throwing items onto the pitch during a football match).
10. Any three from:
    + pressure to win or succeed as an individual
    + pressure from the media or nation to win
    + pressure from coaches to take them in order to increase their chances of winning
    + to gain money or fame as a result of success
    + to improve performance (e.g. via improved fitness, strength, stamina or power)
    + to improve recovery time (e.g. from training; from injury)
    + to increase the ability to train (i.e. for longer or harder)
    + to mask (i.e. cover up) pain
    + to lose weight
    + to level the playing field because of the belief that others are taking PEDs.
11. Any three from the following:
    + PEDs can lead to long term ill health (both physical and/or mental), addiction and over-reliance on PEDs.
    + There are sanctions (i.e. negative consequences) when found guilty (e.g. long-term bans, fines or financial penalties such as the loss of prize money, and the potential loss of sponsorship).
    + PEDs give an unfair advantage against 'clean athletes' who have not taken them.
    + The use of PEDs is cheating/against the rules.
    + PEDs give sport/certain sports a bad name (e.g. cycling and athletics where there is a mistrust of results).
    + PEDs can reflect badly on an individual or nation.
12. 1 mark for the description: information that has to be provided to the 'authorities' (e.g. the UK Anti-Doping Agency [UKAD]) by a select group of named elite athletes.
    Athletes must (1 mark for one of the following):
    + provide information about their location (outside of competition)
    + be available for a 60-minute timeslot in an agreed place every day

+ understand that three missed tests in a year results in a sanction.

13 Any two from:
   + the sport could gain a negative reputation/image
   + the sport could see a reduction in income and/or sponsorship
   + spectators may mistrust results or question whether they are watching 'clean' and fair sport
   + people may mistrust events as a result of large numbers of positive tests or scandals (e.g. among 100 m Olympic sprinters and Tour de France cyclists)
   + there may be scepticism about all performers in a sport if there are lots of PED cases in that sport
   + young people may be put off taking up the sport meaning that it suffers from decreased participation.

14 Any two from:
   + create partnerships (e.g. the cross-organisation work between WADA and National Anti-Doping Organisations [NADOs])
   + carry out random drugs testing and observe WADA's Whereabouts Rule
   + hand out harsher punishments for those found guilty of taking illegal PEDs (e.g. long-term bans)
   + remove sponsorship or National Lottery funding from athletes found guilty of taking PEDs
   + educate performers on the (health) risks of taking PEDs and ways to create an ethically fair/drug-free approach to competing (e.g. via initiatives like '100% Me').

15 Total 2 marks (1 mark for sports initiative and 1 mark for correctly linked value)

Sports initiative	Values promoted
Sport Relief	Citizenship/tolerance and respect
ECB's 'Chance to Shine' campaign	Team spirit/inclusion
FIFA's 'Football for Hope' campaign	Inclusion
Sport England's 'This Girl Can' campaign	Inclusion
The FA's 'Respect' campaign	Fair play/tolerance and respect
Kick It Out!	Inclusion/tolerance and respect

16 Total 3 marks (1 mark for each correct match)
   1 – b
   2 – a
   3 – c

17 Use the following indicative content alongside the level of response grids when marking extended (8 mark) questions:

Respect: fostering and developing a culture of mutual respect across people of different ages, genders, ethnicities and social backgrounds.

Excellence: developing a positive attitude in order to try and achieve your best (e.g. trying to gain a personal best at the championships regardless of medal potential).

Friendship: showing the value of sharing and teamwork (e.g. friendships between athletes of different nations at the closing ceremonies).

Courage: overcoming obstacles and barriers in order to meet your goals (e.g. participating and competing at the Paralympics after life-changing injuries or illnesses).

Determination: overcoming barriers and sticking to your goals, in the belief that persistence will ultimately be rewarded (e.g. overcoming early poor performance in a competition to recover and perform well).

Inspiration: motivating others through hard work and achievement (e.g. inspiring the next generation by acting as a positive role model and demonstrating the need for a positive work ethic in order to succeed).

Equality: ensuring the inclusivity of all groups including ethnicity, ability, gender and age groups (e.g. allowing participants to observe different dress codes that are sensitive to their religious beliefs).

The benefits of positive sporting behaviour at major events include:
+ performers are on show at high-profile events resulting in high levels of media coverage
+ performers act as role models to many millions of people watching worldwide
+ performers' dedication and commitment inspires others to participate
+ a potential increase in the popularity of sport
+ a positive image of the sport improves the reputation of the sport as well as the host country or city
+ it could help the sport attract funding
+ it makes the games fairer and promotes sportsmanship
+ it increases enjoyment for both fans/spectators and participants
+ it celebrates diversity between cultures
+ it generates national pride
+ it creates a safe environment for sport.

Topic area 3

1. a One-off events are held in a host city once in a generation.
   b Regular events are held in a different city each year, but could return to a previous location after a few years.
   c Regular and recurring events are held each year at the same venue/city.
2. Any three from:
   + the UEFA Champions League Final
   + the Europa League Final
   + the Diamond League Athletics Final
   + the British Open Golf Championships.
3. Any three from:
   + the Asian Games
   + the Olympics/Paralympics
   + the Commonwealth Games
   + the FIFA World Cup (football)
   + World Cups in cricket, rugby league and rugby union, etc.
4. Total 6 marks (1 mark for each correct answer)

Sporting event	One-off	Regular	Regular and recurring
Asian Games	X		
UEFA Champions League Final		X	
FA Cup Final			X
Paralympics	X		
Formula 1 British Grand Prix			X
London Marathon			X

5. Negative pre-event aspects – any three from:
   + very high financial costs when bidding for the event; money could be better spent elsewhere
   + environmental resistance to the transport/infrastructure development necessary in order to host an event
   + possible negative legacy of unused sports facilities if not effectively planned for.

   Positive pre-event aspects – any three from:
   + social benefits – increased recognition of the host nation in the world
   + economic benefits – the economy is stimulated with the expectations of increased investment, trade and tourism
   + job benefits – more jobs are created as the bidding process gets underway
   + transport/infrastructure development – via plans for the development of air, road and railway systems
   + sporting developments – via plans for new sporting facilities to increase participation from grassroots to elite level.

6. Any four from:
   + very high costs of staging the event can lead to financial issues or debt (e.g. to a National Governing Body)
   + a possible legacy of unused facilities if not effectively planned for
   + a focus on rugby (e.g. via increased media coverage/role models) so other sports may miss out on promotion
   + possible divisions in society between areas of the country where the matches are staged and areas where they are not
   + possible local objections to hosting (e.g. due to forced relocation of businesses to build facilities or to make transport improvements)
   + increased congestion or pollution in areas hosting matches during the tournament.
7. Positive financial effect – one from: increased employment (e.g. jobs in construction); increased investment in the area/facilities brings in more money; commercial benefits (e.g. from sponsors or external investment); increase in tourism leading to an increase in spending that boosts local businesses and the local economy.

   Negative financial effect – one from: new jobs may only be temporary; the country may not be able to afford to host an event and it might put them into debt; the expense of bidding/hosting diverts money from other areas; tourism benefits are mainly localised.

   Positive effect on facilities – one from: new sporting facilities may be developed; new facilities can be used after the event.

   Negative effect on facilities: if not properly planned for, facilities may be underused or not used at all after the event.
8. Total 5 marks (1 mark for each correct answer)

Positive aspects	Negative aspects
Increased tourism	Possible over-crowding; increased litter; increased pollution
Increased job opportunities	Jobs created may only be short-term and/or recruited from outside an area
Development of new sports facilities	Possible underuse of facilities after the event if not appropriately planned for
Increased participation in sport	Increased participation may only be short-lived; sports may struggle to cope with increased numbers due to lack of clubs, coaches and facilities
Improved morale	If performers don't do well, morale may go down

9 Any four from:
  + improved social infrastructure
  + improved social cohesion/national pride
  + increased interest in sport from the country/nation
  + increased media coverage, which creates more interest in sport across the country
  + increased tourism/financial benefits
  + increased short-term employment during the event.

10 Use the following indicative content alongside the level of response grids when marking extended (8 mark) questions:
  + **Sports facilities are improved or developed/built**
    World class sporting venues will be developed for major sporting events:
    - resulting in better facilities for the nation after the event/facilities can be used after the event by elite athletes and recreational performers alike (e.g. Beijing's Bird Nest developed into a winter wonderland; Olympic stadium being converted into a multi-purpose venue/football stadium; Eton Manor being converted into a hockey and tennis centre)
  + **Greater national interest in sport; increased participation/ increased popularity in sports as a result of watching sports performers/elite role models (i.e. a greater national interest in sport)**
    For example, increased popularity in rugby union following the Rugby World Cup in 2015
    - Hosting major sporting events increases spectatorship and participation rates (e.g. increased popularity in rugby union post rugby work cup in 2015; increased participation rates in cycling following the London 2012 Olympics; increased spectators for women's tennis following the success of Emma Raducanu in the 2021 US Open)
    - Increase in role models (e.g. Mo Farrah winning gold at London 2012)
  + **Increased funding allocated to sports**
    - Sports attract more funding in the lead up to a major sporting event from the government grants/ national lottery/ sponsorship deals/ Sport England/UK Sport (e.g. increased funding for women's rugby union)
    - Funding can be used to develop grass roots participation e.g. British Cycling organising the Sky Ride programme
  + **Increase in media coverage of sport (TV stations bid to cover different sports, e.g. BBC and Sky TV)**
    - Participation rates may increase in some sports due to increase media coverage during major sporting events (e.g. increase in BMX participation due to London 2012)
    - Increased spectators because of additional viewing platforms (e.g. more people watched netball on Sky following England's success in the Commonwealth Games, which was shown on TV)
  + **Investment in infrastructure**
    Increased investment in the development/improvement of the transport system to help cope with the increased numbers of visitors/spectators expected to visit before, during and after the event; increased investment in the local area (i.e. regeneration)
    Investment in local transport/ road networks may result in economic regeneration of the area e.g. the Javelin railway to the London Olympic Stadium (e.g. better transport network)
  + **Increase commercial benefits for local businesses**
    Businesses may benefit due to increase customer base /new businesses are created (e.g. travel companies increasing sales)
  + **Creation of jobs/ employment opportunities**
    A range of jobs are created resulting in a stronger economy (e.g. increased construction/retail/hospitality) – staff for hotels and restaurants/security jobs (NB: many of these may only be short-term)
  + **Increased tourism (direct and indirect tourism)**
    Direct tourism involves visitors visiting the host city/country as a result of attending the major sporting event, whilst indirect tourism is that which results from visitors visiting the host city/country after the event having been made aware of it via global media coverage
    Increased tourism during an event generates revenues in economic sectors such as retail, hospitality and accommodation (e.g. money spent in local hotels/bars/restaurants). Increased revenue from merchandise sales, etc. Increased revenue from tourists visiting other local attractions (e.g. more people may visit Mount Fuji or Hiroshima whilst in Japan for the Rugby World Cup)
    Tourism may increase after the event (e.g. returning to the country for a holiday at a later date)
  + **Admission charges/ticket sales**
    Revenue is generated by ticket sales to view matches/events during a major sporting event (e.g. 64 matches during the football World Cup generates lots of revenue through ticket sales)
  + **Facilities may generate income**
    - Admission charges from public use after the games will generate revenue (e.g. Velodrome being open to the general public after Olympic Games)

Topic area 4

1. b
2. d
3. c
4. Any three from:
   + lobby for and receive funding
   + Sport England
   + grants/government funding
   + membership/national affiliation fees
   + subscription/match fees
   + National Lottery funding/UK Sport
   + media/TV rights
   + income from sponsorship/advertising
   + donations
   + merchandising
   + admission charges/ticket sales
   + NGB initiatives.
5. Any four from:
   + organisation of competitions/tournaments
   + providing funding to clubs
   + providing resources and guidance on coaching/coaching awards
   + providing advice on facilities/sources of funding for facility development
   + providing advice on safeguarding
   + training and providing officials
   + providing insurance to members
   + providing a central handbook/contact details for local clubs an individual may wish to join.
6. Any two from:
   + advice on equipment (e.g. safety equipment)
   + advice on venues
   + advice on surfaces (e.g. information about artificial surfaces).
7. Any three from:
   + providing national performance centres
   + organising national performance squads, elite training camps and access to elite coaching
   + training high-level coaches
   + training high-level officials
   + providing funding support to elite level performers (e.g. squads/teams)
   + developing Talent ID schemes
   + providing a clear progression pathway to elite level sport.
8. Any four from:
   + promote participation
   + promote volunteering/coaching opportunities
   + increase media coverage
   + set up targeted initiatives (e.g. school sport participation)
   + attract funding (e.g. via sponsorship).
9. Any two from:
   + provide funding directly
   + provide advice on funding sources (e.g. Sport England, National Lottery)
   + offer technical advice
   + provide legal advice.
10. Any three from:
    + promotion
    + sources of insurance
    + technical issues (e.g. playing surfaces)
    + sources of funding
    + access to coaching/officiating awards
    + details of leagues and competitions to join in with
    + details of health and safety policies within their sport (e.g. safeguarding).
11. Total 6 marks (1 mark for role, 1 mark for supporting example). Any three from:
    + promoting participation (e.g. via schemes for schools, equal opportunities policies, media coverage/exposure – press releases/social media coverage)
    + organising competitions and tournaments (e.g. FA – Premier League; FA Cup)
    + amending existing rules and applying disciplinary procedures (e.g. the FA disciplinary procedures/rule changes)
    + developing coaching and officiating infrastructure (e.g. netball coaching/officiating awards; detailing levels to progress through)
    + developing policies/initiatives (e.g. anti-doping policies [ECB])
    + promoting positive etiquette/fair play (e.g. the FA's 'Respect' campaign).
12. Use the generic extended question level of response grids alongside the following indicative content to guide marking on 8 mark questions:

    Lobby for (apply for) funding sport in the UK
    + NGBs are responsible for providing advice and support to members looking to access funding to improve provision.
    + NGBs/sports clubs require money/income in order to operate.

    There are a number of ways NGBs can lobby for/get funding, as illustrated by the following list of potential sources:
    + UK Sport for elite performer investment
    + Sport England
    + grants/government funding
    + membership/national affiliation fees
    + subscription/match fees
    + National Lottery/UK Sport funding

- media/TV rights
- income from sponsorship/advertising (e.g. via corporate partners such as the FA and Vauxhall; Rugby League and First Utility)
- donations
- merchandising
- admission charges/ticket sales
- NGB initiatives (e.g. Football Foundation, the United Kingdom's largest sports charity, which channels funding from the Premier League, the FA and the Government to transform the landscape of grassroots sport in England).

Funding distribution:
Having generated lots of income/money, NGBs then have to decide how to spend it (i.e. distribute it).

NGBs distribute their funds to a variety of different sources including the following:
- grants/funding awards to individual performers
- funding to help elite performers compete successfully in international sports events
- funding of grassroots schemes/initiatives (e.g. in sports clubs)
- education/schools
- community engagement
- funding sports venue/facility development
- funding user groups to increase participation in under-represented groups of the community (e.g. minority ethnic groups).

Topic area 5

1. b
2. d
3. d
4. Electrostimulation is the use of electrical impulses to contract muscles in order to help prevent injuries and/or speed up recovery.
5. Negative impacts of technology for a sports performer include:
   - high costs/expense
   - lack of availability to all.
6. Any three from:
   - screens in grounds/stadia
   - (live) media broadcasting
   - instant replays (live on TV/in grounds)
   - VAR
   - Hawkeye
   - HOT Spot
   - TMO
   - Third Umpire
   - DRS
   - statistical information (e.g. on player performance).
7. Any four from:

Examples of technology	Positive effects
Big screens in the ground/stadium	Easier to view participant activities (e.g. in athletics you can view field events and the start and finish of track events from different positions in the stadium)
Media broadcasting	Sport is shown worldwide so fans can see live matches anywhere in the world and support their team; broadcasters can change the timing of events so fans can access them at prime time
Pause/live TV replays	Instant replays are used to help see what has happened and help spectators to understand decisions reached
VAR	Spectators can also review play to help understand the decision reached
Technology providing statistical information on sport	Tracking player movement supports an increased understanding of player and team performance (e.g. time in possession, number of successful passes or shots on target)

8   Any three from:
    + improves bone density; increases muscle power; improves circulation
    + reduces joint pain/delays onset of muscle soreness
    + alleviates stress
    + boosts metabolism
    + maintains cartilage integrity where weight-bearing activities are difficult to undertake.

9   Any three from:
    + officials using technology can be wrong, or they can rely too much on technology
    + people may lose respect for the official's decision being final
    + technology can change the nature of the sport
    + costs limit technology to certain events
    + breaks in play can be disruptive for performers and fans if they take too long.

10 Any four from:
    + technology has helped ensure the correct decisions are made, reduced controversy and increased performer confidence in decisions reached
    + it has helped increase communication between officials as decisions are made
    + it has decreased pressure on officials and the extent of post-match criticism
    + it has helped to improve the accuracy of timings/movements
    + it creates excitement in the crowd as decisions are awaited
    + in some sports, players are allowed to officially 'review or challenge' decisions (e.g. cricket's Decision Review System [DRS] or the 'challenge' system in tennis).

11 'For' goal-line technology; any two from:
    + it is fairer; judgements are based on facts not perceptions
    + it leads to excitement while waiting for the judgement/decision
    + it takes the pressure off referees and cuts down on human error.
    'Against' goal-line technology; any two from:
    + it takes away the chance element of the sport
    + enjoyment is deceased because of the lack of dispute/controversy
    + it takes up too much time, causes too many delays or interrupts the flow of the game
    + it can still be wrong or inaccurate
    + it changes the nature of the game as a sport.

12 Use the generic level of response grids as well as the indicative content below when marking such extended (8 mark) questions:
    Modern technology has made sport fairer as follows:
    + **Officiating – increased accountability and correct decisions:** technology helps officials to make more accurate decisions (e.g. via instant replays and reviews of decisions in sports such as tennis, football, rugby and cricket).
    + **Measurement/better timing devices:** technology provides more accurate measuring devices/more accurate timing systems.
    + **Overturning:** technology allows officials to reverse decisions which have been found to be incorrect (e.g. off-sides in football; LBWs in cricket).
    + **Reduction in cheating:** technology improves the detection of foul play/gamesmanship, sometimes via retrospective action and a panel reviewing incidents a match official might have missed.
    + **Drug testing:** an increased investment in technology improves doping detection (e.g. athlete biological passports).
    + **Inclusion:** technology allows athletes with disabilities to be included in sporting activities/events (e.g. via adaptive equipment).
    Modern technology has also made sport 'less fair' in a variety of different ways, including:
    + increased pressure on officials due to exposure and constant media scrutiny of their decisions
    + the creation of new drugs/masking agents to avoid detection and allow performers to continue cheating
    + inequality as some performers cannot afford the new technologies being developed so access to modern technology may be limited and not available at all levels of competition.

Glossary

100% Me The UKAD's education and information programme to help athletes retain an ethically fair, drug-free approach to sport. 37

Adapted sports equipment Any equipment that has been modified to accommodate people with physical differences or disabilities. 58

Aerodynamic Having a shape that reduces the drag from air moving past. 60

Anti-doping Preventing the use of illegal PEDs. 54

Assistive technology Products that support and assist people with disabilities or restricted mobility to perform functions they would not otherwise be able to. 58

Barriers to participation Things that stop or limit an individual from participating in or developing their skills in a physical activity or sport. 11

Benefits Positive outcomes which result from hosting a major sporting event. 43

Boccia A target sport, involving soft leather balls, that is played indoors by athletes who need high levels of support. 20

Central contracts Elite Player Squad (EPS) agreements. 54

Chance to Shine A national charity that aims to give all children the opportunity to play, learn and develop through cricket (e.g. through 'Chance to Shine Schools' and 'Chance to Shine Street'). 33

Chance to Shine Street A scheme which gives children and young adults in inner-city areas the opportunity to play cricket. It is played with a tapeball (a tennis ball wrapped in electrical tape) and plastic bats, and matches last for just 20 minutes – it's cricket's answer to five-a-side football! 33

Community engagement A way of developing a working relationship between public bodies (such as local councils/ schools) and community groups. 50

Concessions Discounts off full-price admissions for selected groups (e.g. school students). 12

Crèche facilities A nursery where young children are cared for (e.g. during a working day or while their parent is participating in a sport or physical activity at a leisure centre). 16

Cultural norms The rules and expectations of a particular society, based on shared values or traditional beliefs. 14

Culture The rules, customs and beliefs of a particular group or society. 9

DBS The Disclosure and Barring Service is a non-departmental public body of the Home Office of the United Kingdom. A DBS check is carried out to make sure a potential coach has no criminal record relating to safeguarding issues. 52

Direct tourism People who visit a host city or country as a result of attending the major sporting event. 45

Discrimination The unjust treatment of different categories of people based on characteristics such as ethnicity, sex or disability. 14

Disposable income The amount of money a person has left over to spend on non-essentials once all their financial commitments have been met (paying food bills, paying the mortgage, etc.). 11

Doorstep Sport Informal sports clubs that aim to provide a variety of sports to impoverished young people – www.streetgames. org/doorstep-sport 22

Drawbacks Negative outcomes which result from hosting a major sporting event. 43

Economically disadvantaged Someone who does not have enough income to meet basic needs and qualifies for state-organised benefits. 9

Electrostimulation The administration of electric current in specified doses to organs or systems of an organism in order to stimulate the action of the organs or systems. 64

Ethnic group A social group that has a common national or cultural tradition. 9

Etiquette The unwritten rules concerning player behaviour. 35

Excellence When performers strive to be the very best they can in their chosen activity and work with maximum effort. 30

FA 'Respect' The FA's 'Respect' programme was launched in the 2008–09 season following a build-up of behavioural problems in the National Game. 33

Football Foundation The United Kingdom's largest sports charity, which channels funding from the Premier League, the FA and the Government to transform the landscape of grassroots sport in England. 55

Futsal A variation on association football (soccer) played on a hard court with a smaller, low-bounce ball. 26

Gait analysis An evaluation of someone's style of walking or running. 60

Check your understanding and progress at www.hoddereducation.co.uk/myrevisionnotes

Gamesmanship Bending the rules and/or stretching them to their absolute limit in order to gain an advantage in sport. 35

Gender A term used to describe the characteristics of men and women which are socially constructed. 9

GPS (Global Positioning System) A space-based navigation system that provides information about location and time. 60

Hoist A device used to support the lifting and moving of individuals, which enables access to physical activities such as swimming. 20

Hypoxic chamber A sealed room in which the oxygen content of the air is reduced to simulate being at altitude. 59

Indirect tourism People who visit a host city or country after the event having been made aware of it via global media coverage. 45

Infrastructure The basic physical and organisational structures and facilities (e.g. buildings, roads and power supplies) needed for the operation of a society or enterprise. 43

Innovation A new method, idea or product. 58

Inspired Facilities A scheme which focused on making it easier for local community and volunteer groups to improve and refurbish sports clubs or transform non-sporting venues into modern grassroots sport facilities. 53

International A major sporting event involving participants and spectators from two or more countries. 40

Kick It Out English football's equality and inclusion organisation, it works throughout the football, educational and community sectors to challenge discrimination, encourage inclusive practices and campaign for positive change. Kick It Out is at the heart of the fight against discrimination for everyone who plays, watches or works in football. 33

Korfball A ball sport with similarities to netball and basketball played by two teams of eight players (four male and four female), with the aim of throwing the ball into a net. 26

Legacy That which is left behind. 43

Marginal gains Small improvements to performance (which can often be the difference between winning and losing at elite level). 58

Montreal Olympics The 1976 Summer Olympics, officially called the Games of the XXI Olympiad, was an international multi-sport event in Montreal, Canada, in 1976, and the first Olympic Games held in Canada. 46

Motion capture analysis The process of recording and then analysing the movement of objects or people. 65

National Governing Bodies (NGBs) Independent, self-appointed organisations that govern their sports through the common consent of their sport. 48

One-off Held in a host city once in a generation. 39

Oxygen tents An enclosure within which the air supply can be enriched with oxygen to aid a patient's breathing. 59

Participate/participation Taking part.

Pathways Structured routes for performers to progress through. 54

Prosthetic An artificial body part, such as a limb. 59

Prozone A new computerised video system that allows the tracking of many individuals performing a sporting activity, such as football. It can be accessed by performance analysts as well as fans of individual clubs. 63

Pundit/punditry A knowledgeable person who, via the media, offers their opinion, guidance or commentary on a particular sport. 65

Racism Prejudice, discrimination or antagonism directed against someone of a different race or ethnicity based on the belief that one's own ethnic background is superior. 14

Regeneration The improvement of and appropriate investment in facilities or delivery of services in poor neighbourhoods and the empowerment of local communities in processes aimed at bringing an area 'back to life'. 44

Regular Held in a different city each year but could return to a previous location after a few years. 39

Regular and recurring Held each year at the same venue or city. 39

Religious observances Behaviour in relation to religious customs (e.g. some religious people may not practise sport on certain days of the week, such as Sunday). 14

Retired people Individuals who have withdrawn from their active working life and are no longer employed in an occupation. 9

Role model A person viewed by others as an example to be imitated. 11

Safeguarding Actions taken for the welfare of children to ensure they are protected from harm. 52

Sanction A threatened penalty for disobeying a rule or law in sport. 52

School-club links An agreement between a school and a community-based sports club to work together to meet the needs of young people. 18

Shop window effect The increased status of a country resulting from successful hosting of major global sporting events. 44

Sky Sports The main subscription-based sports channel provider in the UK. 24

Social cohesion The set of characteristics that mean a group is able to function as a unit. 43

Social inclusion Making sure all community groups have an opportunity to participate in sport. 30

Social infrastructure The fundamental services and structures that support the quality of life of a nation or neighbourhood (e.g. transport services such as pedestrian areas or cycle lanes; venues and public spaces for recreation, such as playgrounds, skateboard parks and outdoor basketball courts). 43

Social media Websites and computer program that allow people to communicate and share information via the internet using a computer, tablet or mobile phone. 18

Spectator etiquette The rules or guidelines for spectators at a sporting event. 35

Sport for Good A scheme involving sport to tackle three of the features of poverty: youth unemployment, youth crime, and health and wellbeing inequalities. 22

Sport punditry The provision of expertise (i.e. advice/information) in sport. 11

Stereotypes Widely held but fixed and oversimplified images or ideas of a particular type of person or thing. 13

Street Games A scheme which uses the power of sport to create positive change in the lives of disadvantaged young people across the UK – www.streetgames.org 22

Talent ID The process of recognising current players or performers that have the potential to excel within a sport. 53

Taster sessions Sessions in which you work for free or at a reduced rate to introduce yourself to potential clients (e.g. a fitness class or first introduction to a sport). 12

Terrestrial TV stations Free-to-air TV, such as BBC, ITV, Channel 4 and Channel 5 in the UK. 24

Therapeutic use exemption (TUE) The process by which an athlete can obtain official approval to use a prescribed prohibited substance or method for the treatment of a legitimate medical condition. 54

Tolerance AND respect Accepting and welcoming players from different social backgrounds. 30

UK Anti-Doping Agency (UKAD) The national anti-doping organisation in the UK. 36

User groups A number of people who are classed together with the same interests who use a product (e.g. a fitness class at a sports centre) and may face a variety of barriers to their participation in sports. 9

Values The principles which help you decide what is right and what is wrong. 29

Vibration therapy Also known as 'whole body vibration' (WBV), can involve the use of vibration plates to induce the effects of exercise in the body. 64

Walking football This is an adaptation of association football aimed at getting people aged over 50 involved in playing football. The rules have been adapted: they include no running and allow only limited contact. 15

World Anti-Doping Agency (WADA) A foundation initiated by the International Olympic Committee based in Canada to promote, coordinate and monitor the fight against drugs in sports. 36

World Anti-Doping Code The World Anti-Doping Code is the core document that harmonises (i.e. tries to make the same) anti-doping policies, rules and regulations within sport organisations and among public authorities around the world. 36

Youth Sport Trust A national charity dedicated to building a brighter future for all young people. 49

Youth Sport Trust Athlete Mentors A scheme that involves using some of Britain's most successful athletes to visit schools and inspire young people to get involved in sport – www. youthsporttrust.org 19